First World War
and Army of Occupation
War Diary
France, Belgium and Germany

34 DIVISION
102 Infantry Brigade
Headquarters
1 September 1918 - 31 July 1919

WO95/2461/4

The Naval & Military Press Ltd
www.nmarchive.com
Published in association with The National Archives

Published by

The Naval & Military Press Ltd

Unit 10 Ridgewood Industrial Park,

Uckfield, East Sussex,

TN22 5QE England

Tel: +44 (0) 1825 749494

www.naval-military-press.com

www.nmarchive.com

This diary has been reprinted in facsimile from the original. Any imperfections are inevitably reproduced and the quality may fall short of modern type and cartographic standards.

© **Crown Copyright**
Images reproduced by permission of The National Archives, London, England, 2015.

Contents

Document type	Place/Title	Date From	Date To
Heading	War Diary And Appendices 102nd Infantry Brigade H.Qrs September 1918 Volume XXXIV Vol 33		
War Diary	Cormette	01/09/1918	02/09/1918
War Diary	Petit Remmel	02/09/1918	09/09/1918
War Diary	Miod 65. 75	10/09/1918	13/09/1918
War Diary	El Teb (Miod 65.75)	13/09/1918	14/09/1918
War Diary	Petit Remmel	15/09/1918	22/09/1918
War Diary	El Teb	23/09/1918	28/09/1918
War Diary	N.20c 3.3	29/09/1918	30/09/1918
Operation(al) Order(s)	102nd Infantry Brigade Order No. 238	31/08/1918	31/08/1918
Miscellaneous	March Table-To accompany 102nd Inf. Bde. Order No. 238		
Miscellaneous	Distribution		
Operation(al) Order(s)	102nd Infantry Brigade Administrative Instructions No. 13. To accompany 102nd Brigade Order No. 238	31/08/1918	31/08/1918
Miscellaneous			
Miscellaneous	Ref Map 1/20000 Sheet 28 S.W.		
Operation(al) Order(s)	To Be Acknowledged 102nd Infantry Brigade Order No. 241 App I (c)	03/09/1918	03/09/1918
Operation(al) Order(s)	Infantry Brigade Order No. 240 App I (b)	02/09/1918	02/09/1918
Miscellaneous			
Operation(al) Order(s)	102nd Infantry Brigade Order No. 241	03/09/1918	03/09/1918
Miscellaneous			
Operation(al) Order(s)	102nd Inf. Bde. Order No. 242	05/09/1918	05/09/1918
Operation(al) Order(s)	102nd Infantry Brigade Order No. 245	07/09/1918	07/09/1918
Operation(al) Order(s)	102nd Infantry Brigade Order No. 243.	08/09/1918	08/09/1918
Miscellaneous	Amendment No.1 to 102nd Infantry Brigade Order No. 243	08/09/1918	08/09/1918
Operation(al) Order(s)	102nd Infantry Brigade Order No. 242	07/09/1918	07/09/1918
Miscellaneous	102nd Infantry Brigade Warning Order.	13/09/1918	13/09/1918
Operation(al) Order(s)	102nd Infantry Brigade Order No. 244	14/09/1918	14/09/1918
Operation(al) Order(s)	102nd. Infantry Brigade Order No. 235 244	15/09/1918	15/09/1918
Operation(al) Order(s)	102nd Infantry Brigade. Brigade Order No. 245		
Operation(al) Order(s)	To All Recipients of Brigade Order 246	18/09/1918	18/09/1918
Operation(al) Order(s)	All recipients of O.O. No. 246-	18/09/1918	18/09/1918
Miscellaneous	Warning Order.	18/09/1918	18/09/1918
Operation(al) Order(s)	102nd Infantry Brigade Order No. 246	18/09/1918	18/09/1918
Miscellaneous	Table "A"-To accompany 102nd Inf. Bde. Order No. 246		
Miscellaneous	1/4th Cheshire Regt	17/09/1918	17/09/1918
Operation(al) Order(s)	102nd Infantry Brigade Order No. 247 App I	19/09/1918	19/09/1918
Operation(al) Order(s)	102nd Infantry Brigade. Brigade Order No. 248 App I-J	20/09/1918	20/09/1918
Operation(al) Order(s)	102nd Infantry Brigade Order No. 249 App IX	21/09/1918	21/09/1918
Miscellaneous	Table "A"-To accompany 102nd Inf. Bde. Order No. 249 App IX		
Operation(al) Order(s)	102nd Inf. Bde. Order No. 241	03/09/1918	03/09/1918
Operation(al) Order(s)	102nd Infantry Brigade Order No 241	03/09/1918	03/09/1918
Miscellaneous	Second Phase		
Miscellaneous	Artillery Operation-First Phase.		
Miscellaneous			

Operation(al) Order(s)	102nd Infantry Brigade Order No. 250 App I-L	27/09/1918	27/09/1918
Operation(al) Order(s)	102nd Infantry Brigade Order No. 251. App I-M.	28/09/1918	28/09/1918
Operation(al) Order(s)	102nd Infantry Brigade Order No. 252. App I-N	20/09/1918	20/09/1918
Operation(al) Order(s)	102nd Infantry Brigade Order No. 253. App I O	20/09/1918	20/09/1918
Miscellaneous	March Table "A" Starting Point, Oosttaverne Cross Roads , O. 21.b.5.8.		
Miscellaneous	Cover for Documents. Nature of Enclosures.		
War Diary	War Diary And Appendices 102nd Infantry Brigade H.Qrs October-1918. Volume XXXV Vol 34		
Miscellaneous	102 Bde H.Q 19	01/11/1918	01/11/1918
War Diary	Wytschaete	01/10/1918	02/10/1918
War Diary	Houthem	02/10/1918	02/10/1918
War Diary	Blegnaert Fm	03/10/1918	07/10/1918
War Diary	Hollebeke.	08/10/1918	12/10/1918
War Diary	De Voorststraat. Cabt.	13/10/1918	14/10/1918
War Diary	(De Voorststraat Cabt) Sheet Fm Q.1.d.93	14/10/1918	14/10/1918
War Diary	Q.9.a.1.1.	14/10/1918	16/10/1918
War Diary	Johnston's Farm.	17/10/1918	19/10/1918
War Diary	Lauwe	19/10/1918	19/10/1918
War Diary	Aelbeke	19/10/1918	19/10/1918
War Diary	St Anne	20/10/1918	23/10/1918
War Diary	U.1.d.4.3.	23/10/1918	27/10/1918
War Diary	St Anne	28/10/1918	28/10/1918
War Diary	Oyghem	29/10/1918	30/10/1918
Miscellaneous	102nd Infantry Brigade. Reinforcements received, October 1918	00/10/1918	00/10/1918
Miscellaneous	102nd Infantry Brigade,-Casualties-October 1918	00/10/1918	00/10/1918
Miscellaneous	Ref Map Sh.29 1/40000		
Operation(al) Order(s)	102nd Infantry Brigade. Order No. 254. App I	02/10/1918	02/10/1918
Operation(al) Order(s)	102nd Infantry Brigade Order No. 258	07/10/1918	07/10/1918
Operation(al) Order(s)	102nd Infantry Brigade Order No. 258.	07/10/1918	07/10/1918
Miscellaneous	102nd Infantry Brigade Summary Of Operations. Appendix XV.	12/10/1918	12/10/1918
Operation(al) Order(s)	102nd Infantry Brigade Order No. 255	02/10/1918	02/10/1918
Operation(al) Order(s)	102nd Infantry Brigade Order No. 257	05/10/1918	05/10/1918
Diagram etc	Visual by Lucas Lamp 2 Shutters between Bde 2 Bns. to be arranged later		
Miscellaneous	Bde Intelligence off Ts 66/32	00/10/1918	00/10/1918
Miscellaneous	102nd Infantry Brigade Instructions No. 1.	10/10/1918	10/10/1918
Miscellaneous	Addendum No. 2 To 102nd Infantry Brigade Instructions. No. 1.	11/10/1918	11/10/1918
Miscellaneous	B Infantry Dispositions for The Attack.		
Miscellaneous	Appendix "A"		
Miscellaneous	102nd. Infantry Brigade Instructions Number 2.	11/10/1918	11/10/1918
Miscellaneous	Addendum No. 1 to 102nd. Infantry Brigade Instructions No. 1.	11/10/1918	11/10/1918
Map	Identification Trace for use with Artillery Maps		
Miscellaneous	102nd. Infantry Brigade Instructions No. 3.	11/10/1918	11/10/1918
Operation(al) Order(s)	102nd Infantry Brigade Order No. 259 App IV	11/10/1918	11/10/1918
Miscellaneous	102nd Infantry Brigade Instructions No. 4	13/10/1918	13/10/1918
Operation(al) Order(s)	102nd Infantry Brigade Order No 260	14/10/1918	14/10/1918
Operation(al) Order(s)	102nd Infantry Brigade Order No 261	15/10/1918	15/10/1918
Operation(al) Order(s)	102nd Infantry Brigade Order No. 261.a. App IV	15/10/1918	15/10/1918
Miscellaneous	102nd Infantry Brigade Warning Order	15/10/1918	15/10/1918
Operation(al) Order(s)	102nd Infantry Brigade Order No. 261 App VII	19/10/1918	19/10/1918
Miscellaneous	Table "A" Starting Point K. 36.b.8.3. (Sheet 28)		

Type	Description	Date From	Date To
Operation(al) Order(s)	102nd Infantry Brigade. Warning Order No. 264.	22/10/1918	22/10/1918
Operation(al) Order(s)	102nd Infantry Brigade Order No. 264 App VIII	22/10/1918	22/10/1918
Operation(al) Order(s)	102nd Infantry Brigade. Warning Order No. 264	22/10/1918	22/10/1918
Operation(al) Order(s)	102nd Infantry Brigade Order No. 264	22/10/1918	22/10/1918
Miscellaneous	Table "A" Starting Point Belleghem Cross Roads N. 27.c.8.1.		
Operation(al) Order(s)	102nd Infantry Brigade Order No. 264	22/10/1918	22/10/1918
Miscellaneous	Table "A" Starting Point Belleghem Cross Roads N. 27.c.8.1.		
Operation(al) Order(s)	102nd Infantry Brigade Order No. 265 App IX	23/10/1918	23/10/1918
Operation(al) Order(s)	102nd Infantry Brigade Order No. 265	23/10/1918	23/10/1918
Miscellaneous	25th Division G.S. 215.	21/08/1917	21/08/1917
Operation(al) Order(s)	102nd Infantry Brigade Order No. 265	24/10/1918	24/10/1918
Operation(al) Order(s)	102nd Infantry Brigade Order No. 265 App X	24/10/1918	24/10/1918
Miscellaneous	102nd Infantry Brigade Instructions No. 1.	24/10/1918	24/10/1918
Operation(al) Order(s)	102nd Infantry Brigade Order No. 267 App XI	26/10/1918	26/10/1918
Operation(al) Order(s)	102nd Infantry Brigade Order No. 267	26/10/1918	26/10/1918
Operation(al) Order(s)	102nd Infantry Brigade Order No. 268 App XII	26/10/1918	26/10/1918
Operation(al) Order(s)	102nd Infantry Brigade Order No 269 App XIII	27/10/1918	27/10/1918
Miscellaneous	March Table "A" to accompany 102nd Infantry Brigade Order No. 269 Starting Point-Road Junction M.12.d.5.7.		
Operation(al) Order(s)	102nd Infantry Brigade Order No. 269	27/10/1918	27/10/1918
Miscellaneous	March Table "A" to accompany 102nd Infantry Brigade Order No. 269 Starting Point-Road Junction M.12.d.5.7.		
Operation(al) Order(s)	102nd Infantry Brigade Order No. 270 App XIV	29/10/1918	29/10/1918
Miscellaneous	March Table "A" to accompany 102nd Inf. Bde Order No. 270 Starting Point-Cross Roads B.23.d.6.0.		
Miscellaneous	Table "A" to accompany Brigade Order No. 268 Starting Point, Mill N.35.a.7.6.		
Operation(al) Order(s)	102nd Infantry Brigade Order No. 271 App XV	30/10/1918	30/10/1918
Miscellaneous	Cover for Documents. Nature of Enclosures.		
Heading	War Diary And Appendices 102nd Infantry Brigade H.Q November-1918 Volume XXXVI Vol 35		
War Diary	Harlebeke	01/11/1918	03/11/1918
War Diary	Morseele	04/11/1918	13/11/1918
War Diary	Belleghem	14/11/1918	14/11/1918
War Diary	Celles	15/11/1918	15/11/1918
War Diary	Renaix	16/11/1918	17/11/1918
War Diary	Flobecq	18/11/1918	30/11/1918
Miscellaneous	Op. Order 272 App I	02/11/1918	02/11/1918
Miscellaneous	March Table "A"-To accompany 102nd Inf. Bde. Order No. 272 Starting Point-Layhoek Road Junction N.20.d.7.7.	03/08/1918	03/08/1918
Operation(al) Order(s)	102nd Infantry Brigade Order No. 273 App II	13/11/1918	13/11/1918
Miscellaneous	March Table "A" To Accompany 102nd Infantry Brigade Order No. 273 Starting Point 102nd Infantry Brigade Headquarters Moorseele.		
Operation(al) Order(s)	102nd Infantry Brigade Order NO. 274 App III	14/11/1918	14/11/1918
Miscellaneous	March Table "A" to accompany 102nd Bde. Order No. 274 Starting Point-Cross Roads East of M in Belleghem (St. Tournai)		
Operation(al) Order(s)	102nd Infantry Brigade Order No. 275 App IV	15/11/1918	15/11/1918
Miscellaneous	Table "A" to accompany 102nd Infantry Brigade Order No. 275 Starting Point. Road Junction at Milestone 13 on Tournai-Renaix Road.		
Operation(al) Order(s)	102nd Infantry Brigade Order No. 276. App V	17/11/1918	17/11/1918

Type	Description	Start	End
Miscellaneous	March Table "A"-To accompany 102nd Inf. Bde. Order No. 276		
Miscellaneous	Cover for Documents. Nature of Enclosures.		
Heading	War Diary & Appendices 102nd Infantry Brigade Headquarters December 1918 Volume XXXVII Vol 36		
Miscellaneous	Cover for Documents. Nature of Enclosures.		
War Diary	Flobecq	01/12/1918	12/12/1918
War Diary	Silly	13/12/1918	14/12/1918
War Diary	Soignies	15/12/1918	16/12/1918
War Diary	Haine St. Pierre	17/12/1918	17/12/1918
War Diary	Monceau	18/12/1918	18/12/1918
War Diary	Chatelet.	19/12/1918	19/12/1918
War Diary	Fosse	19/12/1918	31/12/1918
War Diary	Fosse	20/12/1918	20/12/1918
Operation(al) Order(s)	102nd Infantry Brigade Order No. 277 App I	11/12/1918	11/12/1918
Miscellaneous	March Table "A" to accompany 102nd Infantry Brigade Order No. 277 Starting Point-Junction of main road just S.E. Of Ogy Church		
Miscellaneous	Amendment No. 2 to 102nd Infantry Brigade Order No. 278. App II	13/12/1918	13/12/1918
Miscellaneous	Amendment No. 1 to 102nd Infantry Brigade Order No. 278	13/12/1918	13/12/1918
Operation(al) Order(s)	102nd Infantry Brigade Order No. 278	13/12/1918	13/12/1918
Miscellaneous	March Table "A" to accompany Brigade Order No. 278 Starting Point-Road Junctions & Mile S.W. of Silly		
Operation(al) Order(s)	102nd Infantry Brigade Order No. 279 App III	15/12/1918	15/12/1918
Miscellaneous	March Table "A" to accompany Brigade Order No. 279. Starting Point-Haut folis Cross Roads 200 Yards due S. of Kilometer Stone 20 on the Coignies-Roeulx Road.		
Operation(al) Order(s)	102nd Infantry Brigade Order No. 280 App IV	16/12/1918	16/12/1918
Miscellaneous	March Table "A" to accompany Brigade Order No. 280		
Operation(al) Order(s)	102nd Infantry Brigade Order No. 281. App V	17/12/1918	17/12/1918
Miscellaneous	March Table "A" to accompany Brigade Order No. 281 Starting Point-Road Junction 400 Yards South Of L in Dampremy.		
Operation(al) Order(s)	102nd Infantry Brigade.Order No. 282 App VI	18/12/1918	18/12/1918
Miscellaneous	March Table "A" to accompany Brigade Order No. 282		
Heading	War Diary And Appendices 102nd Infantry Brigade Headquarters January 1919 Volume XXXVIII Vol 37		
War Diary		01/01/1919	22/01/1919
Operation(al) Order(s)	102nd Infantry Brigade Order No. 1 App I		
Miscellaneous	Table "Z" to accompany 102nd Infantry Brigade Order No. 1		
Operation(al) Order(s)	102nd Infantry Brigade Order No. 2 App II	27/01/1919	27/01/1919
Miscellaneous	Table "A" to accompany 102nd Infantry Brigade Order No. 2		
War Diary	Wahn	01/02/1919	03/02/1919
War Diary	Lohmar	04/02/1919	07/02/1919
War Diary	Siegburg	08/02/1919	26/03/1919
Miscellaneous	To, Adjutant General, Base.	13/05/1919	13/05/1919
War Diary	Siegburg	01/04/1919	17/04/1919
War Diary	Allner	17/04/1919	30/06/1919
War Diary	Wahn	01/07/1919	31/07/1919

VOLUME XXXIV

WAR DIARY AND APPENDICES

102ND INFANTRY BRIGADE H.QRS.

SEPTEMBER 1918

Edward Hill
Brigadier General
Commanding 102ND Infantry Brigade

VOLUME XXXIV
102 Inf BRIGADE
Ref SH.27 T.28

SEPTEMBER. WAR DIARY or INTELLIGENCE SUMMARY.
(Erase heading not required.)

Instructions regarding War Diaries and Intelligence Summaries are contained in F. S. Regs., Part II. and the Staff Manual respectively. Title pages will be prepared in manuscript.

Place	Date	Hour	Summary of Events and Information	Remarks and references to Appendices
CORMETTE	1st		102nd Inf Bde moved from CORMETTE Camp by march route to LUMBRES Sn and entrained for PROVEN arriving 11.30pm. Advance parties by bus convoy at 9pm. Proceeded by road into camp at PERZEELE night 1/2 inst.	
	2nd		Camp camps No 228 issued SH26 1030 Bde to relieve 107th Bde. Relief completed by 2am 3/9/18. Blonden.	APP 19 SH 26 APP(a)
PETIT KEMMEL	3rd	6pm	Bde Hdqrs moved ...	APP(B)
		6.40pm	102 Inf Bde Rep started to advance with Artillery	
		6.35pm	Enemy replied. Slowing signs of Retiring. Advance under No B4 Coys with Lewis (guns) relief of 102 Rd Coy 1st Bn Cheshire Regt) by 101st Bde.	APP(c)
	4th	6.30	102nd Inf Bde had the help of an Artillery Barrage announced to advance. The advance was repulsed.	

Army Form C. 2118.

WAR DIARY
or
INTELLIGENCE SUMMARY.

(Erase heading not required.)

Ref SH 28 SW.

Place	Date	Hour	Summary of Events and Information	Remarks and references to Appendices
POTIJZE KEMMEL	7		Bde. O/O. No 243 issued with regard to relief of 1/1st Bn. Sherwood Reg'ti: Brigade Boundaries altered to Run: Northern Boundary N1 central N16 D 03 013 D 26. 08 D 3.1. Southern Boundary N1 B 03.3 Road Junction N 22 A 0 2 Road Junction N 2 6 D 0 2. 1/7 Worcesters Regt. relieved 1/1st Sherwood Regt. 1/4 Bn Cheshires Regt. Support 1/1st Hereford Regt Reserve. Relief completed by 7.20pm & 12 Jnd.	(APP 5)
	8	10AM	Bde. aarung order sent out by wire to the effect that Reliere 102 &nd Bde. 103 Bde. would Relieve the 102 & 3 Bde. the day and enemy along the whole Brigade front.	
	9		During the night 8/9th Bn. Patrols was pushed forward from Farmer Trench (N 24 c 2 67) to N 24 C 7.5 to found in esssive of Enemy Newports' near Strickland	

… **WAR DIARY** or **INTELLIGENCE SUMMARY.**

(Erase heading not required.)

Army Form C. 2118.

Ref SH 28 1/20,000
28 SW 1/10,000

Place	Date	Hour	Summary of Events and Information	Remarks and references to Appendices
PETIT KEMMEL	4.9		Successful raid at night. Ran M 23 B 73 then K B in Barrel Dugout, there are so far advances but was established at M 23 C 36 & M 24 A 0 7.	Ref SH 28 1/20,000
				Ref SH 28 1/10,000
	6.9		Bltn. moved to support in relief of 1/8 Chesh Regt & 1/4 Bn (A.M.S) Cheshire Regt. by M.M.G. & T.M. Regt came into use 1/4 R Oxford Regt came into the VIERSTRAAT SWITCH TRENCH. Relief completed by 5 AM 6 & Sept 1918.	
	6.9		The day was quiet except for Artillery activity during the afternoon. Very high patrols were pushed forward into OAK TRENCH & FORMER TRENCH. The Enemy was found to occupy a post of OAK TRENCH having orders to relief of 1/4 R Oxford Regt issued	

Army Form C. 2118.

WAR DIARY
or
INTELLIGENCE SUMMARY. Ref SH 28 SW. 1/20.000

(Erase heading not required.)

Instructions regarding War Diaries and Intelligence Summaries are contained in F. S. Regs., Part II. and the Staff Manual respectively. Title pages will be prepared in manuscript.

Place	Date	Hour	Summary of Events and Information	Remarks and references to Appendices
PETIT KEMMEL	9th		at N24A3.3 - N24A5.2 N24C3.9 and we put NE at FERMER TRENCH (N23D 8.7). Dawn to nightfall 9/10th the Brigade was relieved by the 101st Infantry Brigade, the two being a new by 06.30 10th Inst.	
MAP 65/8 10th			The balance of units were at Ypres. Bn HQ M26.5.75 1/4 Oxford Bn M12.c.25.20 temporary area 1/5 Ox Bn M26.a.05.50 1/1st R.Yorks coys R39A M12 33.6.85 102nd MG M.7.B.11 units spent the day cleaning Equipment	16 August S.2.f 1/10 000
	11th		" " " Cleaning of Equipment	
	12th		Training carried out by all units before relieve of Reserve Brigade issued.	
	13th		Training Continued until Warning order received that the	

WAR DIARY
or
INTELLIGENCE SUMMARY.

Army Form C. 2118.

(Erase heading not required.)

Place	Date	Hour	Summary of Events and Information	Remarks and references to Appendices
EL TRE (M.06.57.6)	3		1/4 Aus. Chahn Regt + 1/2 An. Hereford Regt were relieved two Coys of the 101st Sy Bde. in the night 13/14 Sept	
	14		Moving orders sent to units. Brigade order No. 244 issued confirming order issued on 13th	APP (1)
Petit Remmin	15		1/4 An CHESHIRE Regt + 1/1st An HEREFORD Regt moved into the line in accordance with Bde order No 244. Relief complete by 2am 16/9/18	No 250
	16		Moving order received for the advance spoken to move. Lts EPERLEQUES AREA in to 16th. Junction being at N.29.c.6.4. Moved to N.29.B.8.4	
	17		Brigade order No 245 issued with regard to a move to EPERLEQUES. Brigade moved to PETIT BOIS.	APP (2)

WAR DIARY
INTELLIGENCE SUMMARY

REF GYTENASTE 4:10,000

Army Form C. 2118.

Place	Date	Hour	Summary of Events and Information	Remarks and references to Appendices
PEZIT	REMMANY 17	9.30 p.m.	Officer + 35 O.R. before found at N24.A.40.90 and moved out to the extreme N24.A.90.40 our to the great amount of enemy wire they were unable to form an entry and kept the interior.	
	18th		The day time quiet along the brigade front along which were established at N30.A.24.80 + N24.C.16.35 + a foot was established at the HOTS at N24.C at N24.C.B.36. 10.30 p.m. 18/19 248 idle.	APR.(4)
	19th		102nd Inf Bde adv No 247. Orders were by the 1/7 Oxford Regt would relieve 2/4 R.W. Surrey Regt on the Razon system as follows - 10.30 p.m. During the night took were established at N24.A.90.95 + N24.A.85.95.	G.R.Q.(1)
	20th		The day was spent along the whole brigade front during the night a post was established at N343.90.90.90 102nd external 1/5 Gln Gloster Regt - relieved	47-7(3)

102nd ... No 248 issued 1/5 Gln Glore Regt

WAR DIARY
INTELLIGENCE SUMMARY

Army Form C. 2118.

WYTSCHAETE 1/10,000

Place	Date	Hour	Summary of Events and Information	Remarks and references to Appendices
DENY KEMMEL	21st		Two Brigades belonging to the 63rd Div. R.P. Rifles were captured in the craters at M.30A 70.25. 102nd Inf. Brigade moving round to relief of 102nd Inf. Bde. By the 101st Inf. Bde.	APP1(K)
	22		During the Evening patrols were established at M.36C 16.22. M.36A 20.17. N.26.A 20.17. During the night advanced to the 102nd Inf. Bde. line. Relieved by 157th Infle. Brigade Bn. took positions at 102nd Inf. Bde H.Q. EL TIR. 1/4 Ln Chshn Regt M123. 1/7 Chshn Regt SCH ER REG B.SRG. 1/5 Bn Seaforth Regt M17A 102 " L.T.M.B. M17B.	[illegible]
EL TIR	23		Cleaning and training carried out by units	
	24		Ditto and training	
	25			

WAR DIARY or INTELLIGENCE SUMMARY

Army Form C. 2118.

REF KEMMEL 1/10,000

Place	Date	Hour	Summary of Events and Information	Remarks and references to Appendices
EL TEB	26th		Patrols carried out by scouts	
	27th	11.30 PM	Lt. Hereford RSGC carried out a scheme. An alarm signal being located and Enemy Barrage position received owing to attack being carried out. No G.S.1 issued re the alarm 5/pts. Drum 102nd Bde. 5/6 2.50 issued	APP (1)
	28th	At 3.20 AM the bombardment on Ypres was opened to 102nd Bde with line 102nd Bde line Resting on 9.40 AM. There was ref the top as follows Warson Crater by trumpets, 1/10,000 E. Edge of Petit Bois, North Brigestown, N Edge of Bois Quarente, Piccadilly Farm Trench. 1/M BE OR 1/9FR Bde before this order No 951 issued 5/pts E Cheshire Regt were to lk the R=minus sqdn & one under the orders of 5 CE Corps 9 FA Bde.	APP (2)

WAR DIARY or INTELLIGENCE SUMMARY

Army Form C. 2118.

Ref KEMMEL Y
WYTSCHAETE 1/10000

Place	Date	Hour	Summary of Events and Information	Remarks and references to Appendices
EL TER	28th	8.30 (app)	Operation order No 262 issued to 1/1st Bn Monmouth Regt. to move up via Siegfried Avenue and the ravine of 60C - 103 - b - h - bb.	See APPND
Voormezeele	29th		102nd Inf.Bde H.Q. moved up to Regents Dugouts. At 10pm the 1/1st Stafford Regt w/1/1st Battery Regt Exeter at Siegfried under the orders of G.O.C. 103rd Inf. Brigade.	
		30	Brigade at rest. Carrying and Observation Parties supplied but the R.E. supplies miners to Voormezeele to set up.	APP (30)

Signed: [signature]
Brigadier General
Commanding 102nd Inf. Brigade

Secret.

Copy No. 13

102nd Infantry Brigade Order No. 238

Ref. map
HAZEBROUCK -
Sheet 5A. 1:100,000.
Sheet 28 - 1:40,000.

31st Aug. 1918.

1. The 102nd Brigade Infantry Group will leave Second Army Training Area CORMETTE on 1st September, 1918.

    (a) Dismounted personnel as under will march to LUMBRES as per attached march table, where they will entrain :-

        (102nd Bde. Headquarters
        (102nd L. T. M. B. ..... : 110
        1/4th Cheshire Regt ...   687
        1/7th Cheshire Regt ...   643
        "A" Coy. 34th M.G.C. ...   135
        102nd Field Ambulance..   15
        1/1st Hereford Regt ...   310

        Remainder of the Brigade will embus at 12 noon 1st Sept. in 17 lorries to be at Cross Roads ¼ mile East of last E in CORMETTE to go to sheet 28 G.32.d.8.3., where they will be met by guides.

    (b) All riding horses under Lieut. WARD 1/1st Bn Hereford Regt. will parade at Cross Roads ¼ mile East of last E. in CORMETTE at 7.0 a.m., and will proceed to ABEELE in one day.

    (c) Transport will proceed by route march under orders of O.C. No. 3 Coy. Train - Starting point Cross Roads 1¼ miles W. of second E in CORMETTE at 10.0 a.m.
        Route - ST. OMER - ARQUES - CASSEL and will stage night 1/2nd Sept. at a place somewhere between CASSEL and STEENVOORDE. This place will be notified later.
        34th Division are arranging to advise O.C. No. 3 Coy. Train direct destination on night 2/3rd Sept.

2. Usual distances on the march will be maintained. All Units will halt independently at ten minutes to the clock hour and resume the march at the hour.

3. <u>Dress</u> - Full marching order. S.D. caps will be worn. Steel helmets will be carried on the back of the pack affixed to the cross braces.

4. Administrative instructions are being issued separately.

5. Troops on arrival at ABEELE Station at 9.0 p.m. will march to RENINGHELST where they will be met by guides who will take them to their destination.

6. Brigade Headquarters will close at CORMETTE at 3.0 p.m. and reopen at time and place to be stated later.

7. Acknowledge.

Issued at 2 a.m. 1-9-18.

A. B. Leake
Captain.
A/ BRIGADE MAJOR.
102nd INFANTRY BRIGADE.

Distribution overleaf

March Table - to accompany 102nd Inf. Bde. Order No. 238

Serial No.	Date	Unit	Starting Point	Time	Route	Station	Time of departure of train.
1.	1st Sept	102nd Bde. H.Q. & 102nd L.T.M.B.	Cross Roads ¼ m. S. of O in CORMETTE.	3.0 p.m.	ETREHEM - Cross Roads ½ m. South-East of M in LEULINGHEM SETQUES - LUMBRES -	LUMBRES	6.0 p.m.
2.	-do-	1/4th Ches.Regt. (687)	-do-	3.6 p.m.	-do-	-do-	-do-
3.	-do-	1/7th Ches.Regt. (643)	-do-	3.10 p.m.	-do-	-do-	-do-
4.	-do-	1/1st H'ford.Regt. (310)	-do-	3.15 p.m.	-do-	-do-	-do-
5.	-do-	"A" Coy. 34th M.G. Battn. (155)	-do-	3.18 p.m.	-do-	-do-	-do-
6.	-do-	102nd Field Amb.	-do-	3.19 p.m.	-do-	-do-	-do-

Distribution -

Copy No. 1 G.O.C.
2 Brigade Major.
3 Staff Captain.
4 1/4th Cheshire Regt.
5 1/7th Cheshire Regt.
6 1/1st Hereford Regt.
7 "A" Coy. 34th M.G. Battn.
8 Bde. Transport Officer.
9 No. 3 Coy. Train
10 Bde. Supply Officer.
11 102 L.T.M.B.
12 Detachment 102nd Fld. Amb.
13 34th Division.
14 41st Division.
15 A.D.M.S. 34th Division.
16 Area Commandant, St. Martin-au-Laert.

17 War Diary
18 File.

102nd Infantry Brigade Administrative Instructions No. 13.

To accompany 102nd Brigade Order No. 238.

Ref. Map.
Sheet 28, 1,40,000.

1. SUPPLIES.
Supplies for consumption 2nd September will be refilled at 8am and delivered direct to units. These rations will be loaded on to the kit lorries and sent under a guard to LUMBRES Station in the case of Entraining troops and in the case of the Embussing troops to the Embussing Point. They will be loaded in bulk on the train and busses. Transport for conveyance of packs and rations will meet the train at ABEELE Station at 9pm. In the case of the troops of 1/1st Bn Hereford Regt. they will meet them at G.32.c, & d, on arrival.

The forage for Saddle Horses doing the journey in one day will be sent on with the kit lorries.

2. LORRIES FOR CONVEYANCE OF BAGGAGE AND KIT.
One lorry per Battalion will be provided (time to be notified). These lorries will travel with the busses conveying the Surplus Personnel. The 1/4th Bn. Cheshire Regt. and the 1/1st Bn. Hereford Regt. will each take ½ the M.G.Coys Officers kits, Mess Kit and mens dixies.

3. L.T.M.B.
The same Transport arrangements as last time will apply regarding the guns and baggage of the L.T.M.B.

4. ADVANCE PARTIES.
Advance Parties as under will travel on the busses:-
Each Battalion - 2 Offrs. 8 O.R.
M.G.Coy.   - 1 Offr.   4 O.R.
Bde. Hqrs.   - 1 Offr.   9 O.R.

5. MEDICAL.
2 Motor Ambulance Cars will follow the column to the Entraining Station.

6. STORES.
All Stores on loan from the Camp Warden will be returned before units leave the Camp and receipts obtained.

7. CAMP.
The Camp will be left scrupulously clean with all tent curtains rolled up.

8. ENTRAINMENT.
An Officer to be detailed by the 1/7th Bn. Cheshire Regt. will report to the R.T.O. at LUMBRES ½ an hour before the arrival of any troops to superintend the Entrainment. He will report to Brigade Hqrs before going for Entraining Strengths of units. The name of this Officer will be notified by 1/7th Bn. Cheshire Regt. to all units and one Officer from each unit will report to him at R.T.Os. office ½ an hour before the arrival of their troops to be acquainted with the allotment of the train.

J. M. M Carlisle
Captain.
Staff Captain.
102nd Infantry Brigade.

31/8/18.

(3)

9. continued.

(iv) The remaining Field Coys. and Pioneers not required for demolition in the rear area will remain at their Headquarter Camps and come under orders of C.R.E. for work on communications, etc., as required.

10. DEFENCE OF REAR LINES.

In the event of a general attack on the front of the II Corps and on those to its right and left meeting with such a measure of success then it would be obviously unwise to expend all available reserves to retain the forward zone, the Division will be responsible for fighting all lines from the front system to the YELLOW (BRANDHOEK) line inclusive, within the Divisional boundaries.

11. Under these circumstances, the following situations will probably develope -

(a) Brigade Headquarters in their present positions.
Two forward Brigades fighting in the front system of defences.
"D" Battalion belonging to the 43rd Inf.Bde., although originally in Divisional Reserve, would probably have been absorbed in fight.
Reserve Brigade disposed with - "A" Battalion in the BROWN Line.
"B" Battalion will move and occupy the GREEN Line North of the Inter-Brigade boundary and "C" Battalion the GREEN LINE South of the Inter-Brigade boundary.

Reserve Coy. 34th Bn. M.G.Corps will detail 8 guns to the Northern Sector and 8 guns to the Southern Sector of the GREEN LINE.

(b) The two forward Brigades driven back, fighting, to the BROWN LINE, or ordered to withdraw behind it. The Headquarters of the LEFT Brigade moves to A.22.c.5.0. Headquarters of the RIGHT Brigade moves to A.23.a.2.8. Headquarters of the Reserve Brigade at G.6.a.2.4. takes over responsibility for the defence of the Sector. Artillery Liaison of both broups is established by the attachment of a senior officer from Right Artillery Brigade Headquarters to Brigade Headquarters at G.8.a.3.7. Troops of the original front line Brigades pass through the troops holding the BROWN and GREEN LINES and re-organize behind the YELLOW LINE which will be occupied by one or both Brigades according to the strength and condition of their commands.

(c) The Battalion in the BROWN LINE having covered the withdrawal of the original front line Brigades will remain in occupation of the BROWN LINE, which will be held as an Outpost system for the defence of the GREEN LINE.
If compelled by much superior force it will withdraw fighting as a rearguard and will delay the advance of the enemy to the greatest extent possible.
Machine Guns in the BROWN LINE will act in conjunction with the Officer Commanding the Infantry Battalion (

(d) Unless ordered by the Corps there will be NO retirement from the GREEN LINE which will be defended with the full strength and resources of the Division.
The Brigades in the YELLOW LINE having re-organised will be prepared to take over the Sector of the GREEN LINE or to carry out counter attacks to restore any situation which may arise in accordance with the course of the fighting.

12. ACKNOWLEDGE.

Brigade Major,
102ND INFANTRY BRIGADE.

P.T.O

Copy No.	1.	1/4th Bn. Cheshire Regt.
	2.	1/7th Bn. Cheshire Regt.
	3.	1/1st Bn. Hereford Regt.
	4.	34th Division.
	5.	102nd L.T.M.B.
	6.	Brigade Transport Officer.
	7.	'D' Coy. M.G. Bn.
	8.	101st Infantry Brigade.
	9.	103rd Infantry Brigade.
	10.	43rd Infantry Brigade.
	11.	G.O.C.
	12.	Brigade Major.
	13.	12th Belgian Division.
	14) 15)	War Diary and File.

9

1.
The 10th Infantry Brigade
will relieve the 101st a.d 102nd
Infantry Brigades in the whole
Divisional front to-night.
Relief by 2100. Reliefs will
be completed by [illegible].

2.
The 1/1st Hereford will take
over the left sector at
present held by the 101st
Brigade. The 1/4th Cheshire
will take over the right
sector at present occupied
by the 102nd Brigade.

3.
The OPs in Commanding the
1/1st Hereford and the 1/4th
Cheshire will immediately
get in touch with [illegible]

4. The Battalion will dispose in depth.

5. ...... the .... the Riet switch between the VIERSTRAAT boundary.

6. Battalion ...... Brigade headquarters will ...... as possible, a ...... showing their dispositions.

7. Battalions will take ...... area ammunition dumps, and then ...... as many as possible ...... acquainted with their locations.

8. All movement in the Divisional area east of the SCHERPENBERG - DICKIEBUSCH line, by sections at 100 yds interval, and to the east of RENINGHELST by platoons at 100 yds interval. Transport will conform.

3.

9. Completion of relief will be wired to Brigade Headquarters by the code word "SPOT".

10. Acknowledge.

A R Heath
Captain
A/Brigade Major.
102nd Infantry Brigade

2-9-19.

Issued to:-

1/4th Cheshire Regt.
1/1st — do —
1/1st Hereford —
A Coy. M.G. Btn.
102nd L.T.M.B.
101st Inf Brigade.
103rd Inf Brigade.
34th Div. g.S.

SECRET   COPY   APP I(c)

TO BE ACKNOWLEDGED

102ND INFANTRY BRIGADE ORDER NO 241

3/9/18

1. In accordance with 34th Divisional order No 259 the 102nd Infantry Brigade will continue to advance and capture and consolidate the YELLOW LINE as shewn on attached map

2. Time to be notified later. - date 4/9/18.

3. The 102nd Infantry Brigade plus one Battalion will be formed up in their jumping off positions as shewn on attached map at 4-30 a,m, 4/9/18.

   1/1st Herefords in front on left.
   1/7th Cheshires in front on right
   1/4th Cheshires in support of both Battalions
   4th Royal Sussex in Reserve of 1/4th Cheshires

   Positions shewn on attached map.

4. The Brigade will attack on a two Battalion frontage. Each Battalion on a 2 Company frontage in depth. 2 platoons of each Company in the first wave, one platoon supporting, one platoon reserve. Each Battalion keeping one Company in support to leading platoons and one Company in reserve to act in case of necessity as a flank guard. 1/1st Herefords attacking on left and 1/7th Cheshires attacking on right.

   The 1/4th Cheshires Support
   The 4th Royal Sussex reserve.

5. The 1/4th Cheshires will as soon as the two leading Battalions move forward be prepared to support, but will not move till the two reserve Companies of the two attacking Battalions move forward. If they move forward it will move up and occupy the area vacated by the two attacking Battalions where it will remain till instructions are issued by G.O.C. Brigade.

6. The 4th Royal Sussex (Reserve) will remain in its present position.

7. As soon as position is captured the two attacking battalions will reform themselves into defensive formations - carefully watching their flanks. The Herefords immediately getting into touch with the Brigade on their left at approximately N24B 1.9 The 1/7th Cheshires extending to right along yellow line. and getting into touch with the 90th Brigade on right. at about N 36A5.1.

8. The position being consolidated the 4th Cheshires will move up to new line and form up in depth- 2 Companies in front and be prepared to move forward on 2nd phase as follows;-

SECOND PHASE
The 1/1st Herefords and 1/7th Cheshires will hold 1st objective and keep one company at hand each to support the 1/4th Cheshires if necessary these Companies may be used as flank guards ot mopping up parties.

SECRET   COPY

APP I B

INFANTRY BRIGADE ORDER NO.240

Ref.Map
Sheet 28 S.W. 1/20,000

2nd Setemeber 1918

1. The 102nd Infantry Brigade will relieve the 101st and 103rd Infantry Brigades on the whole divisional front tonight 2nd/3rd September. Reliefs will be completed by 4 a.m,.

2. The 1/1st Bn, The Hereford Regiment will take over the left sector at present held by the 101st Infantry Brigade.

X. The 1/4th Bn, The Cheshire Regiment will take over the right sector at present occupied by the 103rd Infantry Brigade.

3. The Officers Commanding the 1/4th Bn, The Cheshire Regiment and 1/1st Bn, The Hereford Regiment will immediately get into touch with their respective Brigades and arrange details and guides

4. The battalions will be disposed in depth.

5. The 1/4th Bn, Cheshire Regiment will occupy the VIERSTRAAT SWITCH between the Divisional boundaries.

6. The battalions will forward to Brigade Headquarters as early as possible a sketch shewing their dispositions.

7. Battalions will take over all Ammunition dumps in their areas and ensure as many as possible are acquainted with their locations.

8. All movemnets in the Divisional area East of the SCHERPENBERG -DICKEBUSCH Line, by sections at 100 yards interval, and to the East of RENINGHELST by platoons at 100 yards interval, transport will conform.

9. Completion of reliefs will be wired to Brigade Heasquarters by the code word "SPOT".

10. ACKNOWLEDGE.

                                        (sd) A.B.LEAKE Capt
                                     A/Brigade Major
2/9/18   102nd Infantry Brigade.

-2-

6. The 1/4th Cheshires will move forward under Artillery by 7-30 a.m. passing through WYTSCHAETE and after capturing will consolidate on EAST of Village protecting their flanks by throwing out flank guards as shewn on MAP and immediately push forward patrols and endeavour to secure the second objective which is the MESSINES - ST ELOY Road East of WYTSCHAETE. It is at this stage the two Companies of the 1/1st Herefords and the 1/7th Cheshires will be ready to move up on LEFT and RIGHT of the 1/4th Cheshires and cove his flank.

O.C. 1/4th Cheshires will detail special mopping up troops who will leave no live ENEMY behind them.

The 1/4th Royal Sussex will when the 1/4th Cheshires move up to attacking position move forward and occupy the position vacated by them and be prepared to support of required.

ARTILLERY CO OPERATION 1ST PHASE.

1. Inaccordance with instructions issued by C.R.A. the artillery will place a barrage at ZERO on a line N.24.cent. to N,29.d.9.4. where it will remain for four minutes and then lift and move forward at a rate of 100 yards in four minutes till it reaches a line running from Central Grid Line N.24. & O.19 till it reaches about N.30.d.0.5. where it will remain for 5 minutes and cease.

2. SECOND PHASE.

At 7-50 a.m. the artillery will place a barrage at line N.30.b.9200 to N 18 d 8.0. remaining for 4 minutes, it will then move in an easterly direction till it reaches line O.20.c.2.1. to O14c3.0 where it will cease. travelling at 100 yds. in 4 minutes.

3. The heavy artillery will co operate by keeping all dangerous zones under heavy fire so long as safe to infantry special attention being paid to WYTSCHAETE.

Machine guns will co operate under order issued by O.C. 34th Machine Gun ~~Battalion~~ Corps Pay spaecial attention to areas on flanks by Artillery Barrage in front of our troops and then flanks, and will place an overhead Barrage over troops on reaching Final objectives for 10 minutes,

They will also pay special attention to any known danger ZONES

11 The O.C. 34th Bn, M.G. Corps will also detail 4 guns to move firward to co operate with each Battalion on consolidation.

STOKES MORTARS will co operate with Battalions according to order issued to each Battalion by him and be prepared to move forward as the line advances.

SIGNALS   O.C. Brigade Signals will take necessary steps to ensure communication from front to rear as Battalions advance-

SPECIAL INSTRUCTIONS

1. O.C. Battalions will ensure that all duties are throoughly understood by their Officers N.C.O's and men.

11 Leaders must follow Barrages closely.

111 Clear and pesitive information must be sent back frequently.

1V Watches will be syncronised by Division with Units at 12-0 midnight.

V Battalions will spare no efforts to gain objectives.

Vl Brigades will syncronise with battalions immediately after by phone. All Adjts. will be at Battalion phones.

Vll Brigade Headquarters will remain at its present place N20D42 during operation.

Vlll ZERO will be at 5-30 a.m.

(signed) EDWARD HILLIAM
Brigadier General
Cdg. 102nd Infantry Brigade

IV   (I) Should the situation change during the night so that Phase 1 will not be necessary the code word "GOTEM" will be sent to all concerned by 4 a.m which will mean that the 1st phase is cancelled but that the 2nd phase will be carried out as per orders-

(II) Should any patrols be forward of Barrage line for Initial Barrage of the code word "GOTEM" is not received O.C. Battalions will make sure that all are brought back to the Jumping off place detailed.

                              (signed EDWARD HILLIAM
                                    Brigadier General
                        Cdg. 102nd Infantry Brigade.

COPY

102ND INFANTRY BRIGADE ORDER NO.241

AFTER ORDER   SEPT 3RD 1918

The second phase of attack is cancelled.

The 1/4th Cheshires will push onward as detailed in Order No.241 IMMEDIATELY the objective of the first phase is gained.

This necessitated the 1/4th Cheshires following close in rear of the two attacking battalions and attempting to push forward to second objective as stated. This Part of the operations will be done without a barrage.

The 1/4th Royal Sussex will move up to 1/4th Cheshires position as soon as they are moved forward

O.C. 1/4th Cheshires will notify O.C. 102nd Brigade if this is clear.

(signed) EDWARD HILLIAM
Cdg, 102nd Infantry Brigade

A.(1).

Should the situation change during the night so that Phase I will not be necessary.

The Code word "GOTEM" will be sent to all concerned by 4·0 a.m. which will mean that the 1st Phase is cancelled but that the Second will be carried out as per orders.

2. Should any patrols be forward of Barrage Line for INITIAL Barrage if the code word "GOTEM" is not received O/C Battalions will make sure that all are brought back to the jumping off place detailed.

Edward Hilliam
Brigadier General
Commdg. 10th Inf. Brigade

Secret
Copy No.

102nd Inf. Bde. Order No 242

Ref. Map
Sheet 28 S.W. 1/20,000

5th September 1918

1/ The 101st Bde will relieve troops of the 102nd Bde on that portion of the Bde front between the Southern Boundary and the new Brigade Boundary described in para. 2 below.

Reliefs to be complete by 5 am. Sept. 6th when G O C 101st Inf. Bde will take command.

2/ New Southern Bde boundary N 25 central — Cross Roads north of LINDENHOEK — STORE Farm and PECKHAM CRATER, both inclusive to right Bde.

3/ (a) 4th Bn. Royal Sussex will come under orders of G.O.C. 101st Bde 8 pm Sept 5th and will relieve 1/7 Cheshires and 1/4 Cheshires South of the boundary described above. All details of relief will be arranged between C.Os. concerned.

(b) 1/1st Bn Hereford Regt will extend their Right Flank to the Southern Bde boundary.

(c) 101st L.T.M.B. will come under orders of G.O.C. 101st Bde. on completion of relief.

4/ On relief 1/4 Cheshires will move into Reserve and be disposed along VIERSTRAAT SWITCH within the Bde boundaries. 1/7th Cheshires will move into Support in N 22 d and N 28 b. between the Bde boundaries having 2 Coys in front and 2 in Support

5/ From 8 pm Sept 5th the Bde Sector will be covered by 190 Bde R.F.A. who will maintain a Liaison Officer at front line Battn Headquarters.

6/ All movements East of SCHERPENBURG – DICKEBUSH line will be by sections at 100ˣ interval.

7 Units of the Bde to acknowledge.

             H. Harler Major
                 BRIGADE MAJOR
                 102ⁿᵈ INF BDE

Issued at 3.30 pm to Signals.

DISTRIBUTION:—

     G.O.C.   Copy No 1.
     Bde Major   "   2.
     Staff Captain   "   3.
     Bde Transport Off   "   4

     Copy No 5 — 1/4ᵗʰ Bn. Cheshire Regt.
     "   6 — 1/7ᵗʰ " Cheshire Regt.
     "   7 — 1/1ˢᵗ " Hereford Regt.
     "   8 — 4ᵗʰ " Royal Sussex Regt.
     "   9 — 102ⁿᵈ L.T.M.B.
     "   10 — 101ˢᵗ L.T.M.B.
     "   11 — 34ᵗʰ M.G. Bn.
     "   12 — 187 Bde R.F.A.
     "   13 — 190 Bde R.F.A.
     "   14 — 90ᵗʰ Inf Bde
     "   15 — 122ⁿᵈ Inf Bde
     "   16 — 101ˢᵗ Inf Bde
     "   17 — 34ᵗʰ Div
     "   18 — War Diary
     "   19 — File

Ref. Map
Sheet 28.S.W.
1:20,000.

SECRET

Copy No.. 13

102nd INFANTRY BRIGADE ORDER No. 243

7th Sept. 1918.

1. Brigade boundaries will be altered tonight as follows :-

   Northern boundary -
   N.1.central - N.13.d.0.5. - O.13.d.2.8. - O.8.d.8.1.

   Southern boundary -
   BEAVER CORNER (N.15.c.5.8.) - Road Junction N.22.a.0.2. - Road Junction N.24.d.0.2.

2. (a) 1/7th Bn. Cheshire Regt. will relieve the 1/1st Bn. Hereford Regt. and troops of the 23rd Middlesex Regt. within the new Brigade boundaries - the Headquarters remaining at N.21.b.7.5. Relief to be complete by 5.0 a.m. 8.9.18.

   (b) 4th Bn. Royal Sussex Regt. will relieve the troops of the 1/1st Bn. Hereford Regt. South of the new Brigade Southern boundary. Relief to be complete by 5.0 a.m.

   (c) On relief the 1/1st Bn. Hereford Regt. will move into Reserve between the KEMMEL-YPRES Road and CHEAPSIDE between the new Brigade boundary.

   (d) 1/4th Bn. Cheshire Regt. will move into Brigade Support and be disposed along the VIERSTRAAT SWITCH within the new Brigade boundary. They will not enter their new area until 9.0 p.m.

   (e) 102nd Light Trench Mortar Battery will have 4 guns in the Forward Area and 4 guns in the VIERSTRAAT SWITCH working with the front and support battalions respectively.

3. Completion of relief will be notified to Brigade Headquarters by the code word "PICQUETS".

   Each Battalion will send this message by messenger dog in addition to the telephone.

4. Battalions will forward a map showing dispositions of their troops as soon as they have been definitely ascertained.

5. Acknowledge.

BRIGADE MAJOR.
Issued to Signals at   p.m.   102nd INFANTRY BRIGADE.

Distribution -
Copy No. 1 G.O.C.
       2 Brigade Major
       3 Staff Captain.
       4 Bde. Sig. Officer.
       5 1/4th Cheshire Regt.
       6 1/7th Cheshire Regt.
       7 1/1st Hereford Regt.
       8 102nd L. T. M. B.
       9 101st Inf. Bde.
      10 103rd Inf. Bde.
      11 123rd Inf. Bde.
      12 190th Bde. R.F.A.
      13 34th Division.
      14 208th Field Co. R.E.
      15 File.
      16 War Diary.

Secret.   Copy No.

102nd Infantry Brigade Order No. 243.

Ref. Map   8th Sept. 1918.
Sheet 28. S.W.
1:20,000.

1. 101st Infantry Brigade will relieve the 102nd Infantry Brigade in the forward area on the night 9/10th September 1918 as under.
    On relief the 102nd Inf. Bde. will move into Divisional Support with Headquarters at old Advanced Divisional Headquarters M.10.d.7.8.

2. (a) 2nd Loyal North Lancs will relieve the 1/7th Bn. Cheshire Regt. who on relief will proceed to N14. All details of the relief will be arranged direct between C.O's concerned. Headquarters of the 2nd Loyal North Lancs will be at PARRAIN FARM.

    (b) On completion of relief the 1/7th Bn Cheshire Regt. will be ready to move forward at short notice to occupy the KEMMEL SYSTEM within the Divisional boundaries.

    (c) Completion of relief of the 1/7th Bn Cheshire Regt. will be notified to these Headquarters by code word "BOMBS".

    (f) The new location of the 1/7th Bn Cheshire Regt. will be notified later.

3. The 1/4th Bn Cheshire Regt. will take over accommodation now occupied by 5th Argyle & Sutherland Highlanders in M.12.d. Their place in the VIERSTRAAT SWITCH will be taken by 2 Companies and Battalion Headquarters 2/4th Queen's Regt.

4. The 1/1st Bn. Herefordshire Regt. will move into the position now occupied by 5th King's Own Scottish Borderers, M.17.b.

5. 102nd L.T.M.B. will be relieved by 101st L.T.M.B. under arrangements to be made direct with O's. C. concerned. On relief they will take over the position occupied by 103rd L.T.M.B.

6. 102nd Bde. Headquarters will close at N.20.d.3.7. at 9.0 p.m. Sept. 9th and reopen at M.10.d.7.8. at the same hour.

9. Acknowledge.

                                                                 Major.
                                                        BRIGADE MAJOR
                                                    102nd INFANTRY BRIGADE.

Distribution -

                Copy No. 1 G.O.C.
                          2 Brigade Major.
                          3 Staff Captain.
                          4 Bde. Signals.
                          5 1/4th Cheshire Regt.
                          6 1/7th Cheshire Regt.
                          7 1/1st Hereford Regt.
                          8 102nd L.T.M.B.
                          9 101st Inf. Bde.
                         10 103rd Inf. Bde.
                         11 34th Division.
                         12 34th M.G. Bn.
                         13 152 Bde. R.F.A.
                         14..... War Diary.
                         15 ..... File.
                         16 ..... 123rd Inf. Bde.

Amendment No. 1
to
102nd INFANTRY BRIGADE ORDER No. 243.

DIV.
G.S.O.1 ✓
G.S.O.2
G.S.O.3
9.9.1918.
L.O.

Reference 102nd Brigade Order No. 243 dated 8.9.1918 -

Para. 2 (b) is cancelled.

Para. 2 (f) Location - M.17.b.

Para. 4   1/1st Bn. Herefordshire Regt. remain in present position.

Major.
BRIGADE MAJOR.
102nd INFANTRY BRIGADE.

Addressed all recipients
of O.O. No. 243.

Ref. Map
Sheet 28.S.W.
1:20,000.

SECRET

Copy No.

WAR DIARY

102nd INFANTRY BRIGADE ORDER No. 242

7th Sept. 1918.

1. Brigade boundaries will be altered tonight as follows :-

   Northern boundary -
   R.1.central - N.13.d.0.8. - O.13.d.2.8. -
   O.8.d.8.1.

   Southern boundary -
   BEAVER CORNER (N.15.c.5.5.) - Road Junction N.22.a.0.2. -
   Road Junction N.24.d.0.2.

2. (a) 1/7th Bn. Cheshire Regt. will relieve the 1/1st Bn.
   Hereford Regt. and troops of the 23rd Middlesex Regt. within
   the new Brigade boundaries - the Headquarters remaining at
   N.21.b.7.8. Relief to be complete by 5.0 a.m. 8.9.18.

   (b) 4th Bn. Royal Sussex Regt. will relieve the troops
   of the 1/1st Bn. Hereford Regt. South of the new Brigade
   Southern boundary. Relief to be complete by 5.0 a.m.

   (c) On relief the 1/1st Bn. Hereford Regt. will move into
   Reserve between the KEMMEL-YPRES Road and CHEAPSIDE between
   the new Brigade boundary.

   (d) 1/4th Bn. Cheshire Regt. will move into Brigade
   Support and be disposed along the VIERSTRAAT SWITCH within
   the new Brigade boundary. They will not enter their new
   area until 9.0 p.m.

   (e) 102nd Light Trench Mortar Battery will have 4 guns
   in the Forward Area and 4 guns in the VIERSTRAAT SWITCH
   working with the front and support battalions respectively.

3. Completion of relief will be notified to Brigade
   Headquarters by the code word "PICQUET".

   Each Battalion will send this message by messenger
   dog in addition to the telephone.

4. Battalions will forward a map showing dispositions
   of their troops as soon as they have been definitely ascertained.

5. Acknowledge.

                                        BRIGADE MAJOR.
Issued to Signals at   p.m.   102nd INFANTRY BRIGADE.

Distribution -
Copy No. 1 G.O.C.   9. 101st Inf. Bde.
        2 Brigade Major   10. 103rd Inf. Bde.
        3 Staff Captain.   11. 153rd Inf. Bde.
        4 Bde. Sig. Officer.   12. 196th Bde. R.F.A.
        5 1/4th Cheshire Regt.   13. 34th Division.
        6 1/7th Cheshire Regt.   14. 208th Field Co. R.E.
        7 1/1st Hereford Regt.
        8 102nd L. T. M. B.   15. File.
                                    16. War Diary.

Secret.

102nd Infantry Brigade Warning Order.

GS.272

13th Sept. 1918.

1. The 102nd Infantry Brigade (less 1/7th Bn. Cheshire Regiment) will relieve the 101st Inf. Bde. (less Battalion in Support) in the line on the night of the 15/16th September.

    Full details will be issued later.

2. Units of 102nd Inf. Bde. to acknowledge.

M Carr
Captain.
BRIGADE MAJOR.
102nd INFANTRY BRIGADE.

34TH DIV.
G.S.O.1
G.S.O.2
G.S.O.3

G.O.C. Bde.	Transport Off.	102nd L.T.M.B.
Bde. Major "	Intell. Off.	101st Inf. Bde.
Staff Capt. "	1/4th Cheshire Regt.	103rd Inf. Bde.
Sig. Off.	1/7th " "	34th Division.
	1/1st Hereford Regt.	209th Field Co. R.E.

S.E.C.R.E.T. Copy No. 6

102nd Infantry Brigade Order No. 235 244 (APP(F))

Ref. Map
Sheet 28 S.W. 1:20,000.

14th September, 1918.

1. 102nd Infantry Brigade Warning Order dated 13.9.18 is confirmed.

2. The 1/1st Bn. Herefordshire Regt. will take over the Left Sector and the 1/4th Bn. Cheshire Regt. the Right Sector of the front line.
   Battalions will be disposed with two Companies in the front zone, one in support and one in reserve, in accordance with instructions issued separately. by battalions.
   All details will be arranged between Commanding Officers concerned.

3. The route for relieving troops will be the SCHERPENBERG—LA CLYTTE—KEMMEL Road. Heads of Battalions will pass the starting point — LA CLYTTE Cross Roads — N.7.c.9.9. at the following times :-

   1/4th Bn Cheshire Regt ... 7.30 p.m.
   1/1st Bn Hereford Regt ... 8.30 p.m.
   102nd L. T. M. B. will proceed independently.

   Movement East of the SCHERPENBERG—LA CLYTTE Road will be by ½ platoons at 100 yds. interval.

4. On completion of relief the Support Battalion of the 101st Inf. Bde. will come under the orders of the 102nd Inf. Bde. and the 1/7th Bn Cheshire Regt. which will remain in its present location will come under the orders of the 101st Inf. Bde.

5. All maps, trench stores, work in hand, anti-aircraft defences, will be carefully taken over.
   A map showing dispositions will be forwarded to Brigade Headquarters as soon as possible after relief.
   Instructions with reference to Brigade in Support, stores and work in hand in present area, will be handed over to incoming units.

6. Administrative instructions will be issued separately by the Staff Captain.

7. The taking of overcoats into the line is left to the discretion of Commanding Officers. No packs will be carried.

8. Brigade Headquarters will close at EL TEB and re-open at N.20.d.3.6. at an hour to be notified later.
   G.O.C. 102nd Infantry Brigade will take over Command of the front on completion of relief. by wire.

9. Completion of relief will be reported by Units to Brigade Headquarters by the Code word "EEL".

10. Acknowledge.

W. Carr Captain.
BRIGADE MAJOR
102nd INFANTRY BRIGADE.

Distribution -
Copy No. 1 G.O.C.
2 Bde. Major
3 Staff Captain.
4 Bde. Transport Off.
5 O.C. 102 Bde. Sigs.
6 Bde. Intell. Off.
7 1/4th Ches. Regt.
8 1/7th Ches. Regt.
9 1/1st Hereford Regt.
10 102 L.T.M.B.
11 No. 3 Coy. Train.
12 34th Division.
13 101st Inf. Bde.
14 103rd Inf. Bde.
15 Bde. on Right. (34th Div. front)
16 Bde. on Left. (do do)
17 C.R.A. 34th Division.
18 C.R.E. 34th Division.
19 & 20 War Diary and File.

ADDENDUM NO.1.
to
102nd. INFANTRY BRIGADE ORDER NO. 235.

      Brigade Headquarters will close at EL TEB at 5-0pm. and re-open at N.20.d.3.6. at the same time.

                                         Captain.
                                  BRIGADE MAJOR.
SEPTEMBER.15th. 1918.   102nd INFANTRY BRIGADE.

Addressed to all recipients of Brigade Order No. 235.

SECRET.

102nd Infantry Brigade.

Brigade Order No. 245.   Copy No.

1. A minor operation will be carried out by "B" Company, 1/7th Bn. Cheshire Regiment against PETIT BOIS and the two craters North of the Western edge of the BOIS at ZERO hour to-night, the 17th instant.
Headquarters of "B" Coy, 1/7th Bn. Cheshire Regt. will be established at N.17.d.4.4.
All arrangements will be made by O.C., 1/7th Bn. Cheshire Regt.
Any prisoners and information will be forwarded immediately to 102nd Infantry Brigade Headquarters.

2. In the event of an S.O.S. being sent up between ZERO hour and the time of return of the raiding party artillery covering front will not fire further West than the road running North and South through N.24. b. and d. central.

3. Co-operation will be provided as follows:-

   (a) Artillery will co-operate by usual night firing and will be prepared if S.O.S. is sent up to place barrage along road indicated in para. 2.

   (b) Machine guns will co-operate with bursts of fire on any known hostile M.G. emplacements or any that may be discovered firing on the raiding party, except those in the area to be raided.

   (c) 102nd L.T.M.B. will co-operate by usual night firing on targets known excepting those in the area to be raided.

   (d) Battalions in the line will co-operate by being prepared to give any assistance that may be required by firing the Lewis Gun at any machine guns that may open fire on the raiding party excepting those in the area to be raided.

4. ZERO hour will be at 9-30 p.m.
   Return of the raiding party to our lines will be notified to all concerned by the Code Word "OAK".

5. In addition to above raiding party the 1/4th Bn. Cheshire Regt. will endeavour after dark to establish a Post in the huts in N.24.c. and also to advance their two Left Posts to our original front line in accordance with separate instructions issued to O.C. Battalion concerned.

6. ACKNOWLEDGE.

                                    Captain,
                                    Brigade Major,
                                    102nd Infantry Brigade.

Copies to-
1. G.O.C.
2. Bde. Major.
3. Staff Captain.
4. Bde. I.O.
5. Bde. S.O.
6. 1/4th Bn. Cheshire Regt.
7. 1/7th Bn. Cheshire Regt.
8. 1/1st Bn. Hereford Regt.
9. 102nd L.T.M.B.
10. O.C. 34th M.G.Bn.
11. O.C. "A" Co. M.G. Bn.
12. O.C. "B" Co. "   "
13. C.R.A. 34th Division.
16. 101st Inf. Brigade.
17. 103rd Inf. Brigade.
18. 152nd Brigade R.F.A.
19. 160th   "   "
20. 21st Inf. Brigade.
21. 122nd "   "
22. Artillery Liason Officer.
23. War Diary.
24. File.

To All Recipients of Brigade Order No. 246.

Brigade Order No. 246 is cancelled.

                    [signature]   Captain,
                                Brigade Major,
                          102nd Infantry Brigade.

18/9/1918.

Addressed -

All recipients of O.O. No. 246 -

102nd Infantry Brigade Order No. 246 is ~~cancelled~~.
postponed pending further orders
102nd Infantry Brigade will remain in the line.

                                                        Captain.
                                            BRIGADE MAJOR
18:9:18.   102nd INFANTRY BRIGADE.

T.S. 48/13

To O.C., 1/7th Bn. Cheshire Regiment.
   O.C., 2/4th Bn. Royal West Surrey Regt.
  101st Infantry Brigade) for information.
✓ 34th Division.   )

WARNING ORDER.

The 1/7th Bn. Cheshire Regiment will relieve the 2/4th Batt. Royal West Surrey Regiment VIERSTRAAT SWITCH on the night of the 19th/20th.

Full details will be issued later.

                        Captain,
                        Brigade Major,
                102nd Infantry Brigade.

18/9/1918.

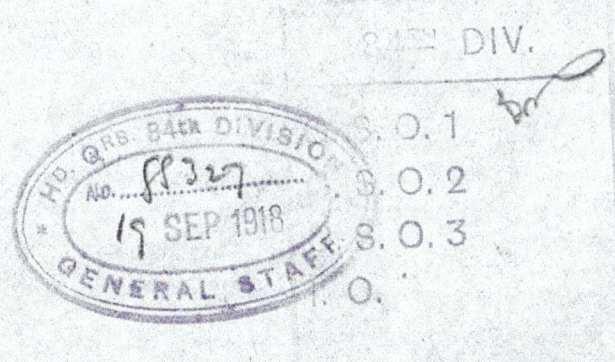

Secret.   Copy No..

102nd Infantry Brigade Order No.. 246

Ref. Maps
Sheets 27 and 28
    1:40,000   18th Sept. 1918.
HAZEBROUCK - 1:100,000.

1 (i)   The 102nd Infantry Brigade (less 1/7th Bn. Cheshire Regt)
        in the line will be relieved by the 101st Infantry Brigade
        (less 2/4th Bn. R.W. Surrey Regt.) on the night of the 18th/19th
        inst.

  (ii) The 4th Bn. Royal Sussex Regt. will relieve the 1/4th Bn
        Cheshire Regt. in the Right Sector and the 2nd Bn. N. Lancs.
        Regt. the 1/1st Bn. Hereford Regt. in the Left Sector.
        101st L.T.M.B. will relieve 102nd L.T.M.B.
        All details will be arranged between Commanding Officers
        concerned.

  (iii) On relief Units will move to the following areas -
        Route - KEMMEL - LA CLYTTE - SCHERPENBERG Rd.

            102nd Inf. Bde. Hd. Qrs.   to   EL TEB.
            1/4th Bn Cheshire Regt..   to   M.12.d.
            1/1st Bn Hereford Regt..   to   FRENCH BANK, M.17.a.1.2.
            102nd L.T.M.B. ....   to   M.17.b.

        Usual intervals will be maintained.
        Small advance parties will be sent from each unit on the
        afternoon of the 18th inst.   They will take over any stores,
        maps from outgoing battalions.

  (iv) All stores, maps, defence schemes, work in hand, will be
        handed over to incoming units.

  (v)   Staff Captain will issue instructions as to Administrative
        arrangements.

  (vi) 102nd Infantry Brigade Headquarters will close at present
        location and reopen at EL TEB at an hour to be notified later.
        Command of the Sector will pass to the G.O.C. 101st Inf.
        Brigade on completion of relief.

  (vii) Units will report completion of relief by wire by code
        word "SOLD".

2. (i) The 102nd Infantry Brigade in the Support Area will be
        relieved by the 103rd Inf. Bde. about 9.0 p.m. on the 19th
        inst.
        All papers, maps, etc. with reference to Brigade in Support
        will be handed over to Units of 103rd Inf. Bde. on arrival.

  (ii) On relief the 102nd Inf. Bde. Group as per margin will move
        to the EPERLECQUES Training Area as under -

102nd
Inf.Bde.
"B" Co.   (a) Dismounted personnel by tactical train entraining at
M.G.Bn.   RENINGHELST Road (G.21.d.central, Sh. 28) at 12 midnight
No. 3 Co   19th/20th inst. detraining at WATTEN on the early
Div.Train.   morning of the 20th inst. in accordance with Table "A"
              attached.   Units will march to the station as soon as
              relieved by Units of 103rd Inf. Bde.
              The Staff Captain will superintend the entrainment.

          (b) Transport by road on the 19th and 20th instant, staging
              at APNEKE on the night 19th/20th instant.
              Transport of the 102nd Inf. Bde. and "B" Coy. M.G. Battn.
              will commence moving at 10.0 a.m. on 19th inst. under
              the orders of the Brigade Transport Officer.

                                           / No. 3 Coy. Train ....

(2)

2.. (continued)

  (ii) (b) - contd.

    No. 3 Coy. Train will join the column Cross Roads L.35.d.2.3. (Sh. 27) on main RENINGHELST--ABEELE Road at 10.30 a.m. when O.C. No. 3 Coy. Train will take command.

    Billets for the night 19th/20th will be obtained from Area Commandant, ARNEKE.

    March to destinations given in Table "A" will be resumed on the morning of the 20th inst. under orders to be issued by O.C. No. 3 Coy. Train.

    Route will be notified later.

  (iii) Instructions regarding Administrative arrangements will be issued by the Staff Captain.

  (iv) Brigade Headquarters will close at EL TEB at an hour to be notified later and re-open at GANSPETTE on arrival.

Acknowledge.

                              M Carr Captain.
                             BRIGADE MAJOR
                       102nd INFANTRY BRIGADE.

Distribution -

Copy No.	
1	G.O.C.
2	Brigade Major
3	Staff Captain
4	Bde. Signalling Off.
5	Bde. Transport Off.
6	1/4th Cheshire Regt.
7	1/7th Cheshire Regt.
8	1/1st Hereford Regt.
9	102nd L.T.M.B.
10	"B" Co. M.G. Bn.
11	O.C. 34th M.G. Bn.
12	34th Div. "G"
13	No. 3 Coy. Train.
14	Bde. Supply Off.
15	101st Inf. Bde.
16	103rd Inf. Bde.
17	Area Comdt. ARNEKE.
18	21st Inf. Bde.
19	122nd Inf. Bde.
20	152nd Bde. R.F.A.
21	160th Bde. R.F.A.
22 & 23	War Diary & File.

Table "A" - To accompany 102nd Inf. Bde. Order No... 246

Ser. No.	Unit	Date	From	To	Train leaves	Remarks
1.	102nd Inf. Bde. H.Q.	19.9.18	EL TEB.	GANSPETTE	To march to WINCHEAST ROAD, G.21.d.central on relief by 103rd Inf. Bde. H.Q.	12 midnight 19th/20th
2.	1/4th Bn. Cheshire Regt.	-do-	SCHUPENBERG AREA.	HELLEBROUCQ	5th Kings Own Scottish Borderers.	-do-
3.	1/7th Bn. Cheshire Regt.	-do-	-do-	EPERLECQUES	8th Scottish Rifles.	-do-
4.	1/1st Bn. Hereford Regt.	-do-	FRENCH BANK	BAYENGHEM.	5th Argyle & Sutherland Hgdrs.	-do-
5.	102nd L.T.M.B.	-do-	M.17.b.	GANSPETTE	103rd L.T.M.B.	-do-
6.	"B" Coy. 54th H.G. Battn.	-do-	BUTTERFLY FARM.	GANSPETTE.	"C" Coy. 34th M.G. Bn.	-do-
7.	No.3 Coy. Train	-do-	B.5.c.7.6. (Sh. 27)	EST MONT.		

Secret.

T. S. 48/7

Ref. Map
HAZEBROUCK - 1:100,000.

1/4th Cheshire Regt.	34th Div. (for information).
1/7th Cheshire Regt.	O.C. "B" Coy. M.G. Bn.
1/1st Hereford Regt.	101st Inf. Bde.
O.C. 34th M.G. Bn.	103rd Inf. Bde.
102nd L.T.M.B.	Bde. Intell. Officer.
No. 3 Coy. Train.	Staff Captain.
Bde. Supply Officer.	Lt. Ward - Off. i/c Bde. L.G. School.

1. With reference to the move back of the 102nd Brigade Group to the EPERLECQUES Training Area, the following arrangements for guides and advance parties will be made.

2. 5 lorries to convoy advance parties of the 102nd Brigade Group to EPERLECQUES will be at RENINGHELST Cross Roads at 8.0 a.m. on the 19th instant.
   Advance parties as under will report to the Brigade Intelligence Officer at these Cross Roads at 7.45 a.m.

	Officers	N.C.O's	Pts	Total
Bde. Headquarters	1	2	2	5
1/4th Cheshire Regt.	1	5	3	9
1/7th Cheshire Regt.	5 (1 per Bn.H.Q. & 1 per Coy.)	5 (1 per Bn.H.Q. & 1 per Coy.)	5 (1 per Bn.H.Q. & 1 per Coy.)	15
1/1st Hereford Regt.	1	5 (1 per Coy.)	3 (1 per 2 Coys.)	9
102nd L.T.M.B.	1	1	-	2
"B" Coy. 34th M.G. Bn.	1	1	-	2
No. 3 Coy. Train	-	1	-	1

   The N.C.O's at present at Bde. Lewis Gun School will be used by Battalions in the line for advance parties.
   Officers or N.C.O's being sent from the Brigade School will be picked up by the lorry at DREEF Cross Roads, L.34.d.1.4. (Sheet 27) Just N. of LAPPE on the main RENINGHELST—ABEELE Road. Brigade Intelligence Officer will arrange.

3. Advance parties will be met in the Square at EPERLECQUES at 12 noon by guides from 103rd Inf. Bde. who will guide them to their new areas as follows :-

1/4th Bn Cheshire Regt	HELLEBROUCQ.
1/7th Bn Cheshire Regt	EPERLECQUES.
1/1st Bn Hereford Regt	DAYENGHEM.
"B" Coy. M.G. Bn	GANSPETTE.
102nd L.T.M.B.	Fme. North of GANSPETTE.
No. 3 Coy. Train	EST MONT.

4. The 102nd Brigade Group will detrain at WATTEN Station on the early morning of the 20th instant where advance parties will meet Units.

5. Each Battalion will also detail one Officer, to take over training facilities and arrangements, to travel with the advance parties. This Officer will make a point of gaining all the information he can from the corresponding unit of the 103rd Inf. Bde. billetted in his respective area as given in para. 3, particularly with regard to tactical schemes and any other special points which the 103rd Inf. Bde. can suggest as the result of their ten days experience in the area. This Officer may be detailed from the Brigade Lewis Gun School.

6 ... Advance parties ..

- 2 -

6. Advance parties of the 103rd Inf. Bde. will arrive at REXINGHELST CROSS ROADS at 7.0 p.m. on the 18th instant. O.C. 1/7th Bn Cheshire Regt. will detail the following guides to be at the Cross Roads by 6.45 p.m. on the 18th inst.

 1 guide for advance party 103 Bde. to guide it to Bde. H.Q. EL TEB.
 1 guide " " 5th K.O.S.B. " " Bn.H.Q., M.12.d.3.4.
 1 guide " " 5th Scottish Rifles " " Bn.H.Q. SCHERPENBERG TUNNEL.
 1 guide " " 5th A. & S.H. " " Bn.H.Q. FRENCH BANK M.17.a.1.9.

O.C. 1/7th Bn. Cheshire Regt. will ensure that reliable guides are sent and that they are acquainted with the locations of the above Headquarters.

O.C. M.G. Battalion will please arrange for guides to meet advance parties of incoming M.G. Coy.

7. The Brigade Lewis Gun School will finish on the 17th inst.. Further orders will be issued as to their move.

8. Acknowledge.

         M Carr
            Captain.
         BRIGADE MAJOR.
17:9:1918.   102nd INFANTRY BRIGADE.
102 B.H.Q.

Secret.   Copy No. 21

102nd INFANTRY BRIGADE ORDER No. 247

Ref. Map
Sheet 28 S.W.   19th September 1918.
1:20,000.

1. The 1/7th Bn Cheshire Regt. will relieve the 2/4th Bn.
    R.W. Surrey Regt. in the KEMMEL SYSTEM on the night 19th/20th
    September.
        All details will be arranged between Commanding Officers
    concerned.

2. Route - SCHERPENBERG - LA CLYTTE - KEMMEL ROAD.

        The head of the 1/7th Bn Cheshire Regt. will pass
    LA CLYTTE Cross Roads at 7.15 p.m. on the 19th instant.
    100x interval will be maintained between ½ Platoons

3. All defences schemes, trench maps, trench stores and
    working parties found by the 2/4th Bn. R.W. Surrey Regt. will
    be taken over.
        Defence scheme for Support area will be handed over to
    incoming unit.
        The two Anti-Aircraft Lewis Gun posts and two Liaison
    posts with flank battalions will also be taken over.
        The usual advance parties will be sent.

4. Completion of relief will be reported by wire to
    Brigade Headquarters by the code word "JAM".

5. Acknowledge.

                                         M Carr Captain.
                                         BRIGADE MAJOR.
                                         102nd INFANTRY BRIGADE.

Distribution -

            Copy No. 1 G.O.C.
                      2 Brigade Major
                      3 Staff Captain.
                      4 Intell. Officer.
                      5 Bde. Signal Officer.
                      6 Bde. Transport Officer.
                      7 1/4th Cheshire Regt.
                      8 1/7th Cheshire Regt.
                      9 1/1st Hereford Regt.
                     10 102nd L.T.M.B.
                     11 2/4th R.W. Surrey Regt.
                     12 34th Division.
                     13 101st Inf. Bde.
                     14 103rd Inf. Bde.
                     15 21st Inf. Bde.
                     16 122nd Inf. Bde.
                     17 152nd Bde. R.F.A.
                     18 160th Bde. R.F.A.
                     19 C.R.E. 34th Division.

                     20 & 21 War Diary & Files.

APP 1-J

102ND INFANTRY BRIGADE.

BRIGADE ORDER
NO. 248.

Secret.

Copy No. 24

20th September 1918.

Reference Map:
Sheet 28. S.W. 1/20,000.

---

1. The 1/7th Battalion Cheshire Regiment will relieve the 1/1st Battalion Hereford Regiment in the Left Sector to-night, 20th/21st instant.
   All details will be arranged between Commanding Officers concerned.

2. Relief will be carried out as soon as possible after dusk.
   The 1/1st Battalion Hereford Regiment will withdraw, on relief, to the KEMMEL SYSTEM. The usual advance parties will be despatched during the day.

3. Defence Schemes, Sector Maps, Stores and Work in hand will be handed over and receipts passed, and lists forwarded to this office as soon as possible after relief.

4. The 1/7th Battalion Cheshire Regiment will not find the working parties 'F', 'G' and 'H' (of Working Party Table forwarded under this Office letter T.S.64/8 of the 19th instant) to-day, 20th instant.
   The 1/1st Battalion Hereford Regiment will find all Working Parties given in above table from the morning of the 21st instant inclusive.

5. Completion of relief will be reported to this office by wire by the Code Word "BAG".

6. ACKNOWLEDGE.

M Carr Captain,
Brigade Major,
102nd Infantry Brigade.

Distribution:
Copy No. 1 G.O.C.
         2 Brigade Major.
         3 Staff Captain.
         4 Bde. Signalling Officer.
         5 Bde. Transport Officer.
         6 1/4th Bn. Cheshire Regt.
         7 1/7th Bn. Cheshire Regt.
         8 1/1st Bn. Hereford Regt.
         9 102nd L.T.M.B.
        10 "B" Coy. M.G.Batt.
        11 O.C., 34th M.G. Batt.
        12 34th Division "G"
        13 No. 3 Company Train.
        14 Bde. Supply Officer.
        15 101st Infantry Brigade.
        16 103rd Infantry Brigade.
        17 21st Infantry Brigade.
        18 122nd Infantry Brigade.
        19 152nd Brigade R.F.A.
        20 160th Brigade R.F.A.
        21 207th Field Company R.E.
        22 208th Field Company R.E.
        23 209th Field Company R.E.

24 & 25 War Diary and File.

Secret.   Copy No. 6

102nd Infantry Brigade Order No. 249

Ref. Map
Sheet 28 1:20,000.

21st Sept. 1918.

1.   The 102nd Infantry Brigade will be relieved in the Right Divisional Sector by the 101st Infantry Brigade on the night 22nd/23rd inst. in accordance with Table "A" attached. All details will be arranged between Commanding Officers concerned.
     The 102nd Infantry Brigade on relief will be in Divisional Reserve.

2.   All stores, maps, defence schemes, work in hand, will be handed over to incoming units.   Message maps forwarded to Units under this office letter T.S. 45/11 dated 18.9.18 and 21.8.18, will be handed over.
     The 1/1st Bn Hereford Regt. will hand over all details regarding Working parties for R.E. to 2nd Bn. R.W. Surrey Regt.

3.   The usual advance parties will be despatched on the morning of the 22nd inst.
     All stores, maps, etc. will be taken over from outgoing units.

4.   The 1/4th Bn. Cheshire Regt. will furnish the A.A. double L.G. post at LA CLYTTE Cross Roads and the 1/7th Bn. Cheshire Regt. the post at CANADA CORNER in accordance with instructions issued under this office letter T.S. 66/12 dated 18.9.18.
     Guns must be posted as soon as possible after arrival in the new area.

5.   The Staff Captain will issue instructions as to Administrative arrangements.

6.   Units will report completion of relief by wire to Brigade Headquarters by code word "SLAB".

7.   Brigade Headquarters will close at N.20.d.3.4. at 7.0 pm and reopen at EL TEB at the same hour.
     Command of Sector will pass to G.O.C. 101st Inf. Bde. on completion of relief.

8.   Acknowledge.

M. Carr
Captain.
BRIGADE MAJOR.
102nd INFANTRY BRIGADE.

Distribution –
Copy No. 1 G.O.C.
         2 Brigade Major.   11. 34th M.G. Bn.
         3 Staff Captain.   12   34th Div. "G".
         4 Bde. Signalling Off.   13   No. 3 Coy. Train.
         5 Bde. Transport Off.   14   Bde. Supply Off.
         6 1/4th Cheshire Regt.   15   101st Inf. Bde.
         7 1/7th Cheshire Regt.   16   103rd Inf. Bde.
         8 1/1st Hereford Regt.   17   21st Inf. Bde.
         9 102nd L.T.M.B.   18   152nd Bde. R.F.A.
        10 "D" Coy. M.G. Bn.   19   160th Bde. R.F.A.
                                       20   C.R.E. 34th Div.

        21 & 22 .. War Diary & File.

Table "A" - To accompany 102nd Inf. Bde. Order No. 249

Ser. No.	UNIT	From	TO	On relief by	Route	Remarks
1	102nd Inf. Bde. Headquarters	N.20.d.3.4.	EL TEB	101st Inf. Bde. Headquarters.	Any	
2	1/4th Bn. Cheshire Regiment	Right Sector	M.12.d.	1/4th Bn. R. Sussex Regt.	KEMMEL — LA CLYTTE Road.	
3	1/7th Bn. Cheshire Regiment	Left Sector	SCHERPENBERG	2nd Bn. L. N. LANCS. R.	–do–	
4	1/1st Bn. Hereford Regt.	Support.	FRENCH BANK M.17.a.1.9.	2/4th Bn. R.W. Surrey Regt.	–do–	
5	102nd L.T.M.B.	Present Location.	M.17.b.	101st L.T.M.B.	–do–	

102nd Inf. Bde. Order 241   Sept 3

After Order   Co 8ᶜ   10 h mm
                      6.30 —

The 2nd Phase of attack is cancelled.

The 1/4 Cheshires will push forward as detailed in order 241 IMMEDIATELY the objective of the 1st Phase is gained.

This necessitates the 1/4 following close in rear of the 2 attacking Battalions & attempting to push forward to 2nd objective — as stated —

This part of the operation will be done without a barrage

The 1/4 Royal Sussex will move up to 1/4 Cheshires position as soon as they move forward.

O/C 1/4 will notify B.G.C. 102nd Bde if this is clear.

Edward Hilliam
Brigadier General
Commdg. 102nd Inf Bde

59

Secret. Copy No. – 9

To be acknowledged

Order
102nd Infantry Brigade, No. 241.

3rd Sept 1918

1. In accordance with 34th Div. Order No. 259, the 102nd Infantry Brigade will continue to advance and capture and consolidate the YELLOW LINE as shown on attached map.

2. Time to be notified later. —
Date 4.9.18.

3. The 102nd Infantry Brigade, plus one Battalion, will be formed up in their jumping off positions as shown on attached map at 4.30 a.m. 4.9.18.

1/1st Herefords in front on Left
1/1st Cheshires in front on Right
1/4th Cheshires in support to both Battalions.
4th R. Sussex in Reserve in Rear of 1/4th Cheshires
Positions shown on attached map.

4. The Brigade will attack on a Two Battalion Frontage. Each Battalion on a Two Company Frontage in depth. Two platoons of each company in first wave, one Platoon supporting, one Platoon Reserve

Each Battalion keeping one Company in support to leading Platoons, and one Company in Reserve to act in case of necessity as a Flank Guard. 1/1st Herefords attacking on Left and 1/7th Cheshire attacking on Right.

The 1/1st Cheshires support
" 4th R. Sussex Reserve.

5. The 1/4th Cheshires will as soon as the Two leading Battalions move forward, be prepared to support, but will not move till the Reserve Coy's of the two attacking Battalions move forward. If they move forward, it will move up and occupy the area vacated by the two attacking Battalions, where it will remain till

instructions are issued by
G.O.C. Bgdes

6/ The 11th Royal Sussex (Reserve) will remain in its present position.

7/ As soon as position is captured the two attacking Battalions will reform themselves into defensive formation, carefully watching their flanks. The Herefords immediately getting into touch with the Brigade on left at approximately N24 D19. The 1/7th Cheshires extending to right along YELLOW LINE and getting into touch with the 90th Brigade on right at about N36 A5.

8/ The position being consolidated the 1/7th Cheshires will move up to the new line and form up in depth. Two Companys in front and be prepared to move forward to second P.T.O

Second Phase.

I. The 1/1st Staffords and 1/1st Cheshires will hold first objective and keep one company in hand each to support the 1/5th Cheshires if necessary. These company's may be used as flank guards or mopping up parties.

II. The 1/5th Cheshires will move forward under artillery at 7.30 am passing through WITSCHAETE and after capturing will consolidate on EAST of village protecting their flanks by throwing out flank guards as shewn on MAP and immediately push forward patrols and endeavour to secure the second objective which is the MISSINES – ST ELOY road east of WITSCHAETE.
It is at this stage the two company's of the 1/1st Staffords and the 1/1st Cheshires will be ready to move up on LEFT and RIGHT of the 1/5th Cheshires and cover his flanks.

(5)

II. (Cont)

- O/C 1/5th Cheshires will detail special mopping up troops who will leave no live ENEMY behind them.

III.

- The 4th Royal Sussex will when the 1/5th Cheshires moves up to its attacking position, move forward and occupy the position vacated by them and be prepared to support if required.

6

Artillery Cooperation – First Phase

- In accordance with instructions issued by C.R.A. The Artillery will place a Barrage at ZERO on a line N24 central to N 29 d 9.4 where it will remain for 4 mts and then lift and move forward at a rate of 100 yds in 4 mts until it reaches a line running from ~~Central~~ CENTRAL grid line N24 and O19 southward along grid between N24 and O19 till it reaches about N30 d 05 where it will remain for 5 mts and cease.

II   2nd Phase

- At 7-30 am the Artillery will place a Barrage at line N30 B 99·00 to N18 d 8·0 remain for 4 mts, it will then move in an easterly direction till it reaches line O20 c 2·1 to O14 c 3·0 where it will cease – travelling at rate of 100 yds in 4 mts.

III.

7.

- The heavy artillery will cooperate by keeping all dangerous ZONES under heavy fire as long as safe to Infantry – special attention being paid to – WYTSCHAETE

Machine Guns will cooperate under orders issued by O/C 31st Btn. M.G. Corps. Pay special attention to areas on flanks of Artillery Barrage in front of our troops and their flanks, and will place an over head Barrage over troops on reaching Final Objectives, for 10 mts.

They will also pay special attention to any known danger ZONES.

II.

The O/C 31st Btn M.G. Corps will also detail 4 guns to move forward to cooperate with each Battalion on consolidation.

STOKES MORTARS will cooperate with Battalions according to orders issued to each Battalion by him, and be prepared to move forward as the Line advances.

SIGNALS. O/C Brigades Signals will take necessary steps to ensure communication from Front to rear as Battalions advance.

SPECIAL INSTRUCTIONS.

I   O/C Battalions will ensure that

(4)

all duties are thoroughly understood by their Officers, N.C.O's and men.

II. Leaders must follow Barrages closely.

III. Clear and positive information must be sent back frequently.

IV. Watches will be syncronised by Division with Units at 12-0 midnight.

V. Battalions will spare no efforts to gain objectives.

VI. Brigades will syncronised with Battalions immediatly after by phone. All Adjts. will be at Battalion phones.

VII. Brigade Headquarters will remain at its present place N 20 d 4.2 during operation.

VIII. ZERO. will be at 5.30 am.

Ross Sutton
Brigadier General.
Commdg. 102nd Inf. Brigade.

SECRET.   Copy No.

102nd INFANTRY BRIGADE ORDER No. 250

Ref. Map Sheet
20 S.W. -
1:20,000.   27th Sept. 1918.

1. The Corps on the left of the 34th Division is attacking the
   enemy position at "H" hour on "J" Day. The 14th Division
will be attacking on the immediate left of the 34th Division.

2. 102nd Infantry Brigade will be in readiness to move from
   H plus 1 hour on "J" Day to allotted positions and to
operate in accordance with extracts from General Staff
Instructions issued to Unit Commanders concerned.

   Units will move on receipt of orders from Brigade
Headquarters.

3. An Officer representative from each Unit will be sent
   to Brigade Headquarters to synchronise watches at an
hour to be notified later.

4. "J" Day will be September 28th.

   "H" Hour will be notified later.

5. Acknowledge.

                                    M Carr
                                                Captain.
102 B.H.Q.   BRIGADE MAJOR.
Issued through Signals   102nd INFANTRY BRIGADE.

    at 7 p.m.
                    Distribution.

                    Copy No. 1 G.O.C.
                           2 Brigade Major.
                           3 Staff Captain.
                           4 Bde. Signalling Officer.
                           5 Bde. Intelligence Officer.
                           6 Bde. Transport Officer.
                           7 1/4th Bn Cheshire Regt.
                           8 1/7th Bn Cheshire Regt.
                           9 1/1st Bn Hereford Regt.
                          10 102nd L.T.M.B.
                          11 34th Division "G".
                          12 101st Inf. Bde.
                          13 103rd Inf. Bde.
                          14 34th Dn. M.G.C.

                        15 & 16 .. War Diary and File.

APP-I-M

102ND INFANTRY BRIGADE ORDER No. 251.

SECRET.

Copy No. 11.

Refcrnc ce Map.
Sheet 28 S.W. 1/20000

1. The 1/7th Batt. CHESHIRE REGIMENT is placed at the disposal of the 101st Infantry Brigade.

The Battalion will move to the KEMMEL SYSTEM in N.21.d. as soon as light permits.

Route and time at the discretion of the Officer Commanding.

Advance parties should proceed to new location forthwith.

The two trench mortars attached will not proceed with the Battalion but will rejoin their battery.

2 ACKNOWLEDGE.

A.B.Leath
Captain,
for Brigade Major
102nd Infantry Brigade.

28/9/1918.

Distribution :-

Copy No. 1   G.O.C.
        2   Bde. Major.
        3   Staff Captain.
        4   Bde. Sig. Officer
        5.   O.C. 1/4th Bn. Cheshire Regt.
        6.   O.C. 1/7th Bn. Cheshire Regt.
        7.   O.C. 1/1st Bn. Hereford Regt.
        8.   102nd L.T.M.B.
        9.   101st Infantry Brigade.
      10.   34th Division "G".
      11.   War Diary.
      12.   File.

APPI-N

102ND INFANTRY BRIGADE ORDER NO.252.   SECRET.
   Copy No. 11.

Reference map
Sheet 28, 1/40000.

1.   The 1/1st Bn. HEREFORD REGIMENT is placed at the disposal of the G.O.C. 103rd Infantry Brigade.

   The Battalion will move as soon as possible in small parties to 103rd Infantry Brigade Headquarters in N.11.a.

   ROUTE : LA CLYTTE - HALLEBAST CROSS ROADS, H.32d.8.1. - VIERSTRAATE.

   Advance parties should be despatched to the 103rd Infantry Brigade H.Q., forthwith.

   The 2 trench mortars attached will not proceed with the Battalion but will rejoin their battery.

2.   ACKNOWLEDGE.

W. Carr Captain,
   Brigade Major,
   102nd Infantry Brigade.

20/9/1918.

Distribution :-

Copy No. 1   G.O.C.
   2   Bde. Major.
   3   Staff Captain.
   4   Bde. Sig. Officer.
   5.   O.C. 1/4th Bn. Cheshire Rgt.
   6.   O.C. 1/7th Bn. Cheshire Rgt.
   7.   O.C. 1/1st Bn. Hereford Rgt.
   8.   102nd L.T.M.B.
   9.   101st Inf. Bde.
   10.   54th Division "G".
   11.   War Diary.
   12.   File.

APPIO

102ND INFANTRY BRIGADE ORDER NO. 255. SECRET.
COPY NO..9..

Ref. Map.
Sheet 28 1/40,000   26/9/1918.

1. The 102nd Infantry Brigade composed of Units as under will move to the area P.9.d. - P.9.c. and d - P.14. and P.15., to-morrow, 1st October, in accordance with March Table "A" attached :-

    102nd Infantry Brigade H.Q.   102nd L.T.M.B.
    1/4th Bn. Cheshire Regt.   No. 3 Company Train.
    1/7th Bn. Cheshire Regt.   'D' Company, M.G. Bn.
    1/1st Bn. Hereford Regt.

2. The following distances will be observed on the line of march -

    Between Platoons, ...   100 yards.
    Between Battalions........   500 yards.
    Between every 6 vehicles.   25 yards.
    Between Unit and its transport. 100 yards.

3. Transport will march in rear of its Unit. The Brigade Transport Officer will arrange for the move of Battalions Transport between SUICIDE CORNER and OOSTTAVERNE Cross Roads.

4. Transport moving from SUICIDE CORNER and Units must not block the WYTSCHAETE - OOSTTAVERNE Road until a Brigade of the 30th Division has cleared OOSTTAVERNE Cross Roads by 10 a.m.

5. Units will halt at 10 minutes to the clock hour.

6. Billetting parties, as ordered by the Staff Captain, will meet Units at bridge P.15.d.8.1., on arrival, and guide them to the areas allotted to them.

7. Instructions as to billetting parties and administrative arrangements will be issued by the Staff Captain.

8. 102nd Infantry Brigade Headquarters will close at REGENT STREET DUGOUTS at 10 a.m., 1st October, and re-open at a time and place to be notified later.

9. ACKNOWLEDGE by wire.

                                    W Carr Captain,
                                            Brigade Major,
                                    102nd Infantry Brigade.

Distribution:-
Copy No. 1.   G.O.C.
         2.   Bde. Major.
         3.   Staff Captain.
         4.   Bde. Signalling Officer.
         5.   Bde. Intelligence Officer.
         6.   Bde. Gas Officer.
         7.   Bde. Transport Officer.
         8.   1/4th Bn. Cheshire Regiment.
        10.   1/7th Bn. Cheshire Regiment.
        11.   1/1st Bn. Hereford Regiment.
        12.   102nd L.T.M.B.
        13.   "D" Coy. M.G. Batt.
        14.   No. 3 Coy. Train.
        15.   Bde. Supply Officer.
        16.   34th Division "G"

17 & 18 War Diary & File.

MARCH TABLE "A".　　　　　　　Starting Point. OOSTTAVERNE Cross Roads, O.21.b.3.8.

Ser.No.	Unit.	From	To	Time head of Unit's Column passes Starting Pt.	Route	Remarks.
1.	1/7th Bn.Cheshire Regiment.	O.21.	Area to be notified at P.13.d.8.1.	10 a.m.	LYTSCHAETE - OOSTTAVERNE Cross Roads - O.17.c.3.7.- O.23.b.0.7.- O.18.c.9.5.- F.20.a.0.2.- Bridge P.13.d.8.1.- F.13.b.5.3.- F.14.b.	Parties of 1/7th Cheshire Regt. & O.C. 16 Hvy Join Battn. after passing Starting Pt.
2.	1/4th Bn.Cheshire Regiment.	O.20.	-do-	10-30 a.m.	-do-	
3.	1/1st Bn.Hereford Regiment.	O.14.	-do-	11-10 a.m.	-do-	
4.	"D" Coy. M.G.Bn.	O.20.	-do-	11-40 a.m.	-do-	
5.	No. 5 Coy. Train.		-do-	11-45 a.m.	-do-	
6.	102nd L.T..B.	REGENT ST. DUGOUTS.	-do-	11-48 a.m.	-do-	
7.	102nd Inf.Bde. H.Q.	-do-	-do-	11-49 a.m.	-do-	

(6392) Wt. W6192/P875 1,500,000 4/18 McA & W Ltd (E 2815) Forms W3091/4.   Army Form W.3091

Cover for Documents.

Nature of Enclosures.

Notes, or Letters written.

VOLUME XXXV

WAR DIARY
AND
APPENDICES

102nd INFANTRY BRIGADE H.Qrs.

OCTOBER - 1918

Murray Hood
LIEUT. COLONEL
COMMANDING 102ND INFANTRY BRIGADE

102 Bde N° 17

Herewith WAR DIARY
for the month of Oct.

1-11-18

H. Peaky
Adjt

WAR DIARY
INTELLIGENCE SUMMARY.
(Erase heading not required.)

Army Form C. 2118.

Refce Maps. SHEET. 28.1/40,000

Place	Date	Hour	Summary of Events and Information	Remarks and references to Appendices
WYTSCHAETE	Oct 1st		102nd Infantry Brigade marched from WYTSCHAETE via OOSTAVERNE & Canal Bridge at HOUTHEM to an area N.E. of HOUTHEM where troops were billeted in German hutments. Brigade HQ. established at TRALEE Fm. Move completed by 14.00. Snow falling by evening at HOUTHEM area.	
	2nd	03.00	Orders received from Division for 102nd Inf Bde to concentrate in area of AMERICA P.6.d & P.7.a. & P.7.c. by 08.00. Bde Order No 254 issued. Limb. commenced moving @ 05.30. Move completed shortly after 08.00. Brigade remained in readiness to support any success gained by the 41st Division. At dusk the 102nd Inf Bde relieved the 122nd & 123rd Inf Bdes with one from a point just S. of GHELUVE to P.8 central with the 1/4th* Bn Cheshire Regt on the left, the 1/7th Bn Cheshire R on the right & the 1/1st Bn Herefordshire Regt in support covered by D Coy M.G. Balln & Artillery of 41st Division &c.	APP I

A6945 Wt. W11422/M1160 350000 12,16 D.D. &L. Forms/C/2118/14.

Army Form C. 2118.

WAR DIARY
or
INTELLIGENCE SUMMARY.
(Erase heading not required.)

REF<u>CE</u> MAPS.
SHEET 28. 1/40,000

Place	Date	Hour	Summary of Events and Information	Remarks and references to Appendices
HOUTNEM	Oct 2nd	1900	Brigade Hd. Qr. took at TRAKLE FARM & Bn. placed at BISQUART F^M O.H.L.	
BISQUART F^M	3rd	0600	Relief of 122nd & 123rd Inf. Bttns completed. Day passed quietly	
" "	4th		Enemy artillery intermittently active and hostile aircraft Observers. No change	
" "	5th		Line was actively patrolled during the night. A minor operation carried out by 1st/4th Cheshire R identified the 126 R.I.R opposite the Dieuvinck Farm	
" "	6th		During the night 5/6th the 1st Batt. Ches R advanced their Cdy 150ft post. The 1/5th Inf. Bth. Came into the line on the left of the 108th Inf. Bth. The 89th Brigade 30 Division was on the right	

Army Form C. 2118.

WAR DIARY
or
INTELLIGENCE SUMMARY.
(Erase heading not required.)

REFCE MAPS.
SH 28. 1/40,000

Place	Date	Hour	Summary of Events and Information	Remarks and references to Appendices
BLEGNAERT FM	Oct. 7	—	No change in situation.	
			Brigade order No 258 issued re relief of 102nd Inf Bde by 101st Inf	APP II
			Brigade. Relief of Brigade complete at 23.00	
HOLLEBEKE	8th	.	Units of 102nd Brigade in relief bivouced in area round ZANDVOORDE	
			Brigade HQ established at 0.6.6.99.	
— " —	9th		Cleaning & Refitting of Units	
— " —	10th		do do Some Training carried out	
— " —	11th	9pm	Brigade Instructions No1. issued to units giving details for forthcoming attack	APP III
			Brigade Order No 259 issued ordering 102nd Inf Brigade to take over portion of Divisional Front	APP IV

Army Form C. 2118.

WAR DIARY
or
INTELLIGENCE SUMMARY.
(Erase heading not required.)

REFCE MAP
SHEET 28. 1/40,000

Place	Date	Hour	Summary of Events and Information	Remarks and references to Appendices
HOLLEBEKE	Oct 12th		At dusk units moved from ZANDVOORDE area & took over the line from portion of 101st Inf Bde from Q.a.a 2270 to Q.q.e.o.5 with the 1/4th Bn Glos R on the left, the 1/1st Bn Cheshire R on the Right & the 1/1st Bn Hereford R in support each Batto kept with its Batto Mortar having the usual 6 Machine Guns & two Stokes Mortars attached to it. Relief complete 23.00	
		0700	Bde HQ closed at HOLLEBEKE & re-opened at DE VOORSTSTRAAT CABT	
DE VOORSTSTRAAT 13th CABT			Night quiet & situation unchanged. Morning quiet. Enemy artillery active M. interpret? active during afternoon.	
		1600	Brigade H.Q. closed at DE VOORSTSTRAAT CABT & re-opened at BA Ma. Ld Q.1 SHEET FARM Q.1.d 7.3	
		7:00	Bombardment with Mustard Gas on Enemy's Heavy Strong localities commenced	

Army Form C. 2118.

WAR DIARY
or
INTELLIGENCE SUMMARY.
(Erase heading not required.)

REFCE MAP SH. 28 1/40,000

Place	Date	Hour	Summary of Events and Information	Remarks and references to Appendices
(DE VOORSTRAAT 14th	OCT			
EAST)		0235.	Line of 1/4th Bn Ches Regt drawn back to conform with barrage line	
		0335.	All units reported in assembly positions ready for advance	
SHEET F.9		04.30.	Gunwalk Counter preparation by enemy artillery few casualties caused.	
Q.I.d.93		0535.	Zero hour. Advance commenced.	
		0600	Capture of 1st objective line 200x W of TERHAND SWITCH reported	
		06.8	Advance resumed	
		0900.	Reports received that final objectives had been gained by assaulting Battalions	
			Bde. H.Q. moved from SHEET F.M. to R.U. for O.9.a.11	
		10.00	Counter attack reported on left of Brigade front. 1/4th Cheshire swung to	
		10.30.	extended front. Coy. of units on right of Brigade on left not having taken objectives, faced back on to line of TERHAND SWITCH.	
			1/1st Bn Herefords R moved to dig defensive line 200x S. of GHELUVE 1/2 Coys	
			Sent to EARTH F.M. to reinforce 1/4th Bn Cheshire R	
			Captures by Brigade during the advance on the day—	
			Prisoners 9 officers, 422 O.R. 77mm guns 2, Heavy M.G. 21, Light M.G. 45, Minenwerfer 13, Light Railway Trucks 200 + large quantities of ammunition	

WAR DIARY or INTELLIGENCE SUMMARY.

Army Form C. 2118.

(Erase heading not required.)

PLACE MAP. BM 28 1/40,000

Place	Date	Hour	Summary of Events and Information	Remarks and references to Appendices
Ogaill	Oct 14th		Approximate casualties during advance to O/from +250 O.R. At dusk the 1/4th Bn. Cheshire R. obtained & organised attack on QUERY FM final objective which was successfully carried out during night. Bge order no 260. Night passed quietly with no hostile artillery fire.	APP V
do	15th		Patrols pushed forward in early morning by 1/4 Bn. Ches R. 1st Bn. Hereford R. & those to enemy from MENIN. 2 Coys of 1/4th Bn. Ches R. moved through MENIN & dug in about BRUGES FARM & the CYCLE TRACK due E. of the town. One Company back of 1/1st Bn. Hereford R. disposed at MARATHON BRIDGE LOCK, & MONGRELS BRIDGE. Front of 102nd Brigade - from MARATHON BRIDGE (excl) to MONGRELS BRIDGE re-adjusted as follows:— 1/1 Battn. Herefords R. set from Batts under O.C. 1/4 Bn. Ches R. 1/4 Batts. Ches R. in Reserve about original Front Line. 1/7th Batts. Ches R. in Support in TERHAND Salient. The Brigade boundary— MENIN (incl.) to round Belf. 705 FARM – BRIDGE at assess MARATHON BRIDGE (all excl.) Bgde order no 261 A.	APP IV

WAR DIARY
or
INTELLIGENCE SUMMARY.
(Erase heading not required.)

Army Form C. 2118.

Ref. MAP SHEET 28 1/40,000

Place	Date	Hour	Summary of Events and Information	Remarks and references to Appendices
Q.Q.a.11	Oct 15th	—	Orders were received to push Patrols a/c HALLUIN if the could be driven without serious fighting during the night. Owing to extreme darkness it was not found possible to cross the river by dark.	
do	16th	—	At dawn Patrols of 1/1st Bn Hereford R. succeeded in closing up river at MARATHON BRIDGE & advancing as far as HALLUIN CHURCH. A bridge from enemy light howitzers was thrown across river at this point. Attempts at same time to cross at the LOCK & MONGREL'S BRIDGE failed. During morning Patrols withdrew from HALLUIN CHURCH but MARATHON BRIDGEHEAD was held till 1900 by company of Scottish Rifles (Jos'd Inf Bde) Under cover of Artillery bombardment & L.G. fire Hereford continued	
		1300.	crossing river in rapt. attack RASCAL'S RETREAT	
		1600.	"A" Coy of 1/1st Bn. Hereford R. had established itself across the river in R.19.a.	
		1700.	Relief of 102nd Inf Bde by 216th Bn London Regt. of 21st Inf Bde commenced.	

Army Form C. 2118.

WAR DIARY
or
INTELLIGENCE SUMMARY.
(Erase heading not required.)

REF. MAP. SH. 28. 1/40,000
SH. 29 "

Place	Date	Hour	Summary of Events and Information	Remarks and references to Appendices
	Oct			
D.9.a.11	16th	2300	Relief of 102nd Inf. Bde completed	
JOHNSTON'S	17th		Brigade in relief billets in farms about K.3.5 & K.3.6.	
FARM		0100	Brigade H.Q. opened at JOHNSTON'S FARM K.36.9.7.2	
			Brigade held in readiness to move at 1 hours notice	
			Day spent in cleaning & refitting units	
do.	18th		Training & refitting having nets ready for continuation of advance	
do.	19th	0400	Brigade order No 261 issued w/c move of 102nd Inf Bde	App VII
		0600	Head of Brigade moved from JOHNSTON'S Ft.	
		0900	Brigade Group assembled with heads of columns on MENIN-MENINGHEM [?]	
			D in Square R.10.11	
			Brigade H.Q. opened at KRUISHOEK	
		0900	Brigade group moved across the LYS by Pontoon Bridge in R.17 + bivouaced W of KAINE. Bde H.Q. opened in farm R.17.a.	

Army Form C. 2118.

WAR DIARY or INTELLIGENCE SUMMARY.
(Erase heading not required.)

Instructions regarding War Diaries and Intelligence Summaries are contained in F. S. Regs., Part II. and the Staff Manual respectively. Title pages will be prepared in manuscript.

Refce. Map SHEET 29 1/40,000

Place	Date	Hour	Summary of Events and Information	Remarks and references to Appendices
LAUWE	Oct 19		At midday 102nd Infantry Brigade Group moved to LAUWE_KNOCK_Sm 5 AELBEKE, arriving at 1600. Brigade H.Q. opened at AELBEKE 16.00.	
AELBEKE	-	1600.	Brigade Group moved to ST ANNE arriving at 1700. Brigade Order No. 261 issued.	APP VII
ST ANNE	20th		Brigade Group remained in ST ANNE Area Training & refitting. Brigade held in readiness to move at short notice. Brigade order No 264 issued re. relief of 124th Inf Bde.	
"	22nd		Commencing at 0940 102nd Infantry Brigade Group moved via BOUEGHEM KNOK & BELLEGHEM to an area just E of BELLEGHEM BOSCH arriving at midday.	APP VIII
"	23rd	1200	Brigade H.Q. opened at T.1.d.4.3. As no circumstances formed, Units of Brigade retained supporting units of 124th Inf Bde during afternoon. Remainder of relief carried out at dusk - completed by 23.00. Front held ran from TUNNEL CANAL held by enemy, ACHTERHOEK_BAVEGHEN KNOK_PEUDERISCH (all inclusive) with 11th Bn Her Regt on (to left 17th Bn Glos Regt on right 17th Bn Glos R in support.	

Army Form C. 2118.

WAR DIARY
or
INTELLIGENCE SUMMARY.
(Erase heading not required.)

REFCE MAP SHEETS 20/1/40 SE

Place	Date	Hour	Summary of Events and Information	Remarks and references to Appendices
U.d.4.3	Oct 23rd	—	Brigade Order No 265 issued giving details as to co-operation by 101st Brigade in attack of 123rd Inf. Brigade E. of the COURCELLES-BONAVIS CANAL. The 9th Bn Leinster R. to give support & Reserve companies to hold line just W. of CANAL TUNNEL.	App IX
do.	24th	0200	Zero hour. Night quiet & securely completed.	
		0300	Constant MG fire across CANAL TUNNEL & 9th Bn Leinster R. unable to advance.	
			At dawn word was received that 123rd Inf Bde have been held up & hostile MG fire.	
		11.59	Conference of C.O. at Bde HQ & scheme for resumption of the attack outlined.	
			Quiet day.	
			Brigade Order No 266 & Instructions No 1 issued. During the night 9th Bn Ches. Regt. attempted to cross river at Locks 3, 4 & 5 but failed.	App X

Army Form C. 2118.

WAR DIARY
or
INTELLIGENCE SUMMARY.

(Erase heading not required.)

Ref. Map
SHEET 29. 1/40,000

Instructions regarding War Diaries and Intelligence Summaries are contained in F. S. Regs., Part II. and the Staff Manual respectively. Title pages will be prepared in manuscript.

Place	Date	Hour	Summary of Events and Information	Remarks and references to Appendices
U.1.d.4.3	Oct 24th		Arrivals of Units in accordance with B.O. 266 + Instr. No 1 Carried out during the night	
do	25th	0845	1/7th Bn rehearsed capture of 2 houses (W.B. Rep.) normal	
		6900	Barrage commenced	
		0904	Zero hour + advance commenced	
		0925	C.O. of 15th ROSB ordered to U.3. to report to right Bn. H.Q. 1/7th Bn Glo. Regt. who had sustained considerable casualties. Enemy resistance to our barrage very slight. 1/7th Bn again failed to cross the canal about lock 5 but succeeded in pushing the enemy from BOSSUYT + establishing two of his Coys N bank of the SCHELDT.	
		1100	M.O.E.s rehearsed capture of 1/4th Bn Glo R + W of cell. 2A 1/7 Bn. Leopards R. McKerry whole area captured. 2nd Bn Midd + R. Wilts were held up on left flank of brigade probably from start of barrage.	

WAR DIARY
INTELLIGENCE SUMMARY

Army Form C. 2118.

REF MAP
Sh 29 1/40,000

Place	Date	Hour	Summary of Events and Information	Remarks and references to Appendices
U.4.3.25.	Oct 25th	1300	1/4th Bn. Ches R. reformed S. of MOEN & advance continued to final objective AUTRYVE & remainder of BUSIGNY captured & photo established along N bank of SCHELDT. Touch obtained with H Bn Ches R. along E flank of CANAL. 4th Bn Hereford R. closed to form defensive flank towards ½. 1 Bn Ches R. & right of 138th Inf Brigade. Night quiet except for considerable shelling of AUTRYVE & MOEN	
-do-	26th		Situation unchanged during night. Enemy batteries active. SHELDT on front of 23rd Inf Bde. Brigade order No 267 issued. Relief of 21st Inf Bde. Brigade order No 268 issued. 4th 21st Inf Bde Area.	APP XI. Move of 102nd Bde Group to STANNE APP XII.

Army Form C. 2118.

Ref. Map
SH 29 1/40,000

WAR DIARY
or
INTELLIGENCE SUMMARY.
(Erase heading not required.)

Place	Date	Hour	Summary of Events and Information	Remarks and references to Appendices
U.1.d.4.3	Oct 27th	0300	Relief by 21st Inf Bde complete. Bn. moved to assembly area U.1.d.4.3 at 0500 hours.	
		10.00	Move of Brigade to ST ANNE ordered.	
			Brigade order No. 269 issued. Bn. to move to OYGHEM-HULSTE Road.	App XIII
ST ANNE	28th	0730	Brigade moved to OYGHEM-HULST Area arriving at 1400	
		14.00	Bde. H.Q. opened at OYGHEM.	
OYGHEM	29th		Battalions refitted & cleaned up.	
			Brigade Order No 270 issued, ordering move to HARLEBEKE	App XIV
-do-	30th	11.28	Brigade commenced move to HARLEBEKE. Bde H.Q. opened at HARLEBEKE	
			Brigade order No 271 issued with resumption of the advance	App XV

102nd Infantry Brigade.
Reinforcements received, October 1918.

	Officers	Other Ranks
1/4th Bn. Ches. Regt.	10	132
1/7th Bn. Ches. Regt.	15	88
1/1st Bn. Herefd. Regt.	5	40
TOTAL.	30	260

102nd Infantry Brigade, - Casualties - October 1918.

	Killed.		Wounded.		Wounded. (Gas)		Missing.	
	O.	O.R.	O.	O.R.	O.	O.R.	O.	O.R.
1/4th Bn. Ches.Regt.	1	37	11	180	2	7	0	5
1/7th Bn. Ches.Regt.	5	34	5	144	0	1	3	31
1/1st Bn. Herefd.Regt.	1	14	2	78	2	7	0	2
102nd L.T.M.B.	0	1	0	2	1	0	0	0
TOTAL.	7	86	18	404	5	15	3	38

Army Form C. 2118.

WAR DIARY
or
INTELLIGENCE SUMMARY.
(Erase heading not required.)

Instructions regarding War Diaries and Intelligence Summaries are contained in F. S. Regs., Part II. and the Staff Manual respectively. Title pages will be prepared in manuscript.

REF MAP
SH 29 1/40,000

Place	Date	Hour	Summary of Events and Information	Remarks and references to Appendices
			Casualties sustained by 102nd Inf. Bde. during October	
			Killed — Off. O.R. — 7 86	
			Wounded — Off. O.R. — 18 404	
			Missing — Off. O.R. — 3 38	
			Gassed — Off. O.R. — 5 15	
			Reinforcements received — Off. O.R.	
	19/11/18			

Murray Moss Lt Col
Comm'dg 102nd Inf Bde.

APP I

102ND INFANTRY BRIGADE ORDER NO. 264.   SECRET.
                                              Copy No.......
                                              2nd October 1918.

Reference Map.
Sheet No. 1/40,000.

1. The 102nd Infantry Brigade and "D" Coy., Machine Gun Batt. will assemble in the AMERICA Area, P.6.d. and Q.7.c. by 8 a.m. on the morning of the 2nd instant.

2. Units will move off in the following order :-
    1/4th Bn. Cheshire Regt at 5-30 a.m.
    1/7th Bn. Cheshire Regt to follow 1/4th Bn. Cheshire Regt.
    1/1st Bn. Hereford Regt to follow 1/7th Bn. Cheshire Regt.
    "D" Coy, M.G. Battalion to follow 1/1st Bn. Hereford Regt.
    102nd L.T.M.B. to follow "D" Coy., M.G. Batt.

    Starting Point – Road Junction P.14.b.4.8.

    Route – Cross tracks P.15.c.1.7. – Road Junction P.10.d.8.4. –
            Road Junction P.11.c.0.0.

    Movement will be by platoons at 100 yards interval.

3. Units will assemble in the Valley in P.6.c. and d., as follows:

    1/4th Bn. Cheshire Regt on the Left in Northern half of P.6.d.
    1/7th Bn. Cheshire Regt on the Right in Southern half of P.6.d.
    1/1st Bn. Hereford Regt.)
    "D" Coy., M.G. Batt.   ) in P.6.c.
    102nd L.T.M.B.   )

    These locations are only approximate and every advantage must be taken of the nature of the ground.

4. Men will be armed with 220 rounds S.A.A.
    Two Stokes Mortars on Pack Mules will be attached to the 1/4th and 1/7th Bns. Cheshire Regiment and four to the 1/1st Bn. Hereford Regiment.

5. A mounted orderly from Brigade Hd.Qrs. will report to each Battalion at the Starting Point. As soon as each Battalion reaches its assembly position and Headquarters located this orderly will be sent to Brigade Headquarters to report dispositions.

6. In the event of the Brigade have to carry out an operation it would assemble in Q.7.c.

7. Battalions will be ready to move on receipt of orders from Brigade Headquarters.

8. Brigade H.Q. will remain at present location, but will move forward later when due notification will be sent to Units.

                                        Captain,
                                        Brigade Major,
                                        102nd Infantry Brigade.

SECRET.

7th October 1918.

102nd INFANTRY BRIGADE ORDER NO. 258

Ref. Map. Sh. 28, 1/40,000.

1. Warning order dated 6/10/18 (B.M.C.21) is confirmed. 101st Infantry Brigade will relieve the 102nd Infantry Brigade on night 7th/8th instant.

2. (a) The 4th Bn. Royal Sussex Regt. will relieve the 1/4th Bn. Cheshire Regiment and 1/7th Bn. Cheshire Regiment in the Forward Zone.
   The 2nd Batt. Loyal North Lancs. Regt. will relieve the 1/1st Bn. Hereford Regiment in Support.
   The 101st L.T.M.B. will relieve the 102nd L.T.M.B.
   All details will be arranged between Officers Commanding Units.

3. The 102nd Infantry Brigade on relief will move to the area P.2.a. and b., J.32 and 33., with Brigade Headquarters at O.6.b.9.9.

4. The Staff Captain will arrange for the following:-

   (a) The allottment of the new Brigade Area to the various units.
   (b) One guide per platoon (to be found from personnel at the Transport Lines) to be at Road Junction P.5.d.7.7. by 7 p.m. and guide outcoming platoons to their new areas.
   (c) Arrange with Units Transports for the move of cookers (hot meals to be ready for outcoming troops), water carts, &c., to the new area, and the dispatch of the necessary transport to bring back kits and stores from the Line.

5. Officers Commanding Units will ensure that outgoing platoons are acquainted with the route to the meeting place with guides, P.5.d.7.7.

6. The Machine Gun Company will remain in its present position.

7. Completion of relief will be reported to Brigade Headquarters by wire by the code word "BELL".

8. The command of the sector will pass to G.O.C. 101st Infantry Brigade on completion of relief.
   102nd Infantry Brigade Headquarters will close at DEVOORSTSTRAAT CABT. on completion of relief and reopen at O.6.b.9.9. at an hour to be notified later.

9. ACKNOWLEDGE.

(sd) M.CARR,
Captain,
Brigade Major,
102nd Infantry Brigade.

Secret.
7th October 1918.

102ND INFANTRY BRIGADE ORDER NO. 258.

Ref.Map.Sh.28, 1/40,000.

1. Warning order dated 6/10/18 (B.M.O.21) is confirmed. 101st Inf Bde will relieve 102nd Inf Bde on night 7/8th instant

2.(a) The 4th Bn. Royal Sussex Regt. will relieve the 1/4th Bn. Cheshire Regt and 1/7th Bn. Cheshire Regt. in the Forward Zone.

The 2nd Batt. Loyal North Lancs. Regt. will relieve the 1/1st Bn. Hereford Regt. in Support.

The 101st L.T.M.B. will relieve the 102nd L.T.M.B.

All details will be arranged between Officers Commanding Units.

3. The 102nd Infantry Brigade on relief will move to the area P.2.a. and b., J.32 and 33., with Bde. H.Q. at Q.6.b.9.9.

4. The Staff Captain will arrange for the following :-

(a) The allotment of the new Brigade Area to the various units.
(b) One guide per platoon (to be found from personnel at the Transport Lines) to be at Road Junction P.5.d.6/67 by 7 p.m. and guide outcoming platoons to their new areas.
(c) Arrange with Units Transports for the move of cookers (hot meals to be ready for outcoming troops), water carts, &c., to the new area, and the dispatch of the necessary transport to bring back kits and stores from the Line.

5.

Sheet 2.

5. Officers Commanding Units will ensure that outgoing platoons are acquainted with the route to the meeting place with guides, P.S.d. &c. ?.?.

6. The Machine Gun Company will remain in its present position.

7. Completion of relief will be reported to Brigade H.Q., by wire by the code word "BELL".

8. The command of the Sector will pass to G.O.C., 101st Infantry Brigade on completion of relief.
102nd Infantry Brigade H.Q. will close at DEVORSTSTRAAT CABT. on completion of relief and re-open at O.6.b.9.9. at an hour to be notified later.

9. ACKNOWLEDGE.

                        Captain,
                          Brigade Major,
                        102nd Infantry Brigade.

APPENDIX XV.

102nd INFANTRY BRIGADE

SUMMARY OF OPERATIONS.

Oct. 12th - Oct. 28th 1918.

Reference Maps
Sheets 28 & 29
1:40,000.

OCT. 12th.

On October 12th the 102nd Infantry Brigade was bivouaced in the area just West of ZANVOORDE with Brigade Headquarters 1,500 yards North-East of HOLLEBEKE.

At dusk Battalions moved forward and commenced taking over the Right Sector of the Divisional front from the 101st Infantry Brigade.

Relief was complete by 23.00 with the Brigade disposed in its battle formations as follows :-

1/4th Bn. Cheshire Regt .. on the left with front extending from South-West corner of GHELUWE in touch with the 103rd Infantry Brigade, to a point 800ˣ due West of QUARANTINE FARM.

1/7th Bn. Cheshire Regt .. on the Right from the right of the 1/4 Bn. Cheshire Regt. to Q.9.d.4.5. in touch with 90th Inf. Bde. of the 30th Division.

1/1st Bn. Hereford Regt .. in Support about Q.2.c.

Each battalion was disposed with 2 Companies in front, one in Support and one in Reserve. 2 Stokes Mortars and one Section of Machine Gunners of "A" Coy. 54th Bn. Machine Gun Corps were attached to each Battalion, the remaining two Stokes Mortars and one Section of Machine Gunners being held in Brigade Reserve.

The Brigade front was covered by the 182nd Bde. R.F.A. and portions of the 160th Bde. R.F.A. supported by a considerable amount of heavy artillery.

Brigade Headquarters opened at DE VOORSTSTRAAT CABT at 16.00 on the 12th.

OCT. 13th.

The night was quiet. The whole Brigade front was patrolled and the enemy found to be on the alert.

1.

Oct 13th.
(continued)

Except for intermittent shelling throughout the day the enemy showed no activity.

Brigade Headquarters closed at DE VOORSTRAAT CABT. at 1800 and moved to battle headquarters at CHEFF FARM Q.1.d.0.3.

At 1900 Artillery covering the front commenced a bombardment of known hostile strong points with Mustard Gas. The night passed quietly and without incident.

Oct.14th.

By 0235 the two front line battalions reported that their line had been re-adjusted to conform with the barrage line in accordance with orders issued, and at 0335 all units reported completion of assembly.

At 0430 the enemy commenced to put down a heavy counter preparation - having been warned, according to prisoner's statements, of our impending attack by noise during assembly of troops - which, however, caused few casualties.

At 0532 our barrage commenced and at H hour 0535 started creeping at the rate of 100" per minute when troops commenced to advance.

The chief opposition was met from Farms and strong points close up to the assembly line and which did not come under the barrage which was put down 500" in advance of the starting line - a distance that proved to be unnecessarily great. Apart from this the opposition was slight.

The two assaulting battalions passed quickly to the first objective, aline running approximately 300" WEST of the TENAND SWITCH.

The advance was greatly assisted by the use of smoke shell by the 103rd. L.T.M.B., many known strong points being effectively dealt with in this manner.

Re-organisation was carried out during the 14 minutes pause on the 1st. Objective, and at 0619 the advance was resumed.

As during the opening phase the opposition was slight, the enemy being more disposed to surrender than to fight.

The final objective of the Brigade - a line running from Q.17.c.9.5. to the MENIN Road at Q.18.d.3.5. - was reached to time and a quick exploitation of this success enabled patrols on the right, accompanied by two guns of the Machine Gun Coy. to push to the EAST of the small village of GHELUVELT; while on the left patrols were sent along the MENIN Road and occupied JOE FARM in an endeavour to obtain touch with the Brigade on the LEFT whose advance had not been so rapid.

OCT. 14th
(continued)

At 09.30 two Companies of the 1/1st Bn. Hereford Regiment were moved from their reserve position to commence a defensive line known as the YELLOW LINE – running 600 to 700X due E. of GHELUWE with the aid of one Section of the 208th Field Coy. R.E.

The thick mist and smoke of the barrage greatly hampered the task of getting back accurate information from the front, while the length of the signal communication likewise delayed the sending of information to the rear and communication with flank Brigades.

At 10.00 Brigade Headquarters moved from SHREW FARM to a Pill box at Q.9.a.1.1.

The forward positions gained by the infantry were maintained until 10.30 a.m. when the enemy opened consistent Machine Gun fire from the direction of MENIN.

The line had become considerably extended both owing to the fact that in the thick fog units had become somewhat confused and that an extension N. of the MENIN ROAD in an endeavour to get into touch with the troops on our left had become necessary. Considerable casualties had also taken place among the leading Officers of the 1/4th Bn. Cheshire Regt.

A counter-attack on the left caused our men to withdraw to the line of the TENIAND SWITCH from QUICK FARM to FLANIE FARM – but the line on the right was maintained except that the two machine guns were compelled to fall back from just E. of GOUGH Village.

As soon as this counter attack was reported at Brigade Headquarters – one of the Companies of the 1/1st Bn Hereford Regt. working on the YELLOW LINE passed to the Command of the O.C. 1/4th Bn Cheshire Regt. and took up a position about EARTH FARM.

Simultaneously the remaining two Companies of this Battalion were moved forward to occupy our original front line.

During the day touch was established with the Scottish Rifles of the 103rd Infantry Brigade at GROUP FARMS.

During the initial advance the chief captures by the Brigade were :-

        9 Officers   422 O.R's.
        2 77 m.m. guns.
      91 heavy M.Gs.
      45 light M.Gs.
      12 minenwerfer.
    500 light railway trucks.

and large quantities of ammunition and other war material.

The casualties sustained by the Brigade amounted approximately to 12 Officers and 250 O.R's.

Oct. 14th
(continued)

At dusk on the 14th orders were issued for the 1/4th Bn Cheshire Regt. to organise an attack with a view to seizing QUERY FARM and the line of the final objective, which was successfully carried out during the night touch being obtained with the 1/7th Bn. Cheshire Regt. just W. of GOUGOU.

The night passed quietly with practically no hostile artillery fire.

Oct. 15th.

Early on the morning of the 15th orders were issued to the 1/4th Bn. and 1/7th Bn. Cheshire Regt. to push forward and occupy MENIN if this could be done without serious fighting. Accordingly patrols of the 1/4th Bn Cheshire Regt. and 1/1st Bn. Hereford Regt. under orders of Officer Commanding the 1/4th Bn Cheshire Regt. pushed forward rapidly and by 09.00 had passed through MENIN with little opposition and established themselves at BRULES FARM and the CYCLE TRACK due EAST of the town.

A strong point was then formed on the CYCLE TRACK by two companies of the 1/4th Bn Cheshire Regt.

One Company of the 1/1st Bn. Hereford Regt. took up a position based on MARATHON BRIDGE – another Company a position based on the LOCK due S. of MENIN and a third Company a position based on HONGRSLE BRIDGE.

At dusk the Divisional front was re-adjusted making MENIN inclusive to the 102nd Infantry Brigade and the junction between Brigade the MARATHON BRIDGE (excl. to 102nd Bde.)

The 1/1st Bn. Hereford Regt. took over the front line and the 1/4th Cheshire Regt. were drawn into reserve and the 1/7th Cheshire Regt. remaining in support.

Col. Drage Commanding 1/4th Bn Cheshire Regt. remained in Command of the front line.

During the night orders were received from the 34th Division for patrols to push across the LYS as far South as LE HALPLAQUE and in conjunction with the 103rd Inf. Bde. who were to operate on the E. of HALLUIN to occupy the town of HALLUIN if unoccupied by the enemy.

It was found possible to do but little during the hours of darkness.

Oct. 16th.

At dawn on the 16th 3 patrols of the 1/1st Bn. Hereford Regt. under S/Lt. Sully of that regiment succeeded in effecting a crossing of the LYS near the MARATHON BRIDGE surprised a machine gun post capturing the gun and putting the team to flight and advanced as far as HALLUIN CHURCH and RUSTY KNOBS. A patrol of the Scottish Rifles also accompanied the party.

OCT. 16th (continued)

A bridge was constructed from old enemy positions in the neighbourhood of MARATHON BRIDGE and one platoon of the 8th Bn. Scottish Rifles got across the river but were prevented from advancing far from the South bank of the river owing to the machine gun fire from the direction of PHONE FARM and from the Church HALLUIN from which our patrols had to withdraw.

An attempt to cross at the LOCK failed owing to the difficulty of the crossing and the activity of the enemy.

At midday a bombardment by field guns and heavy artillery on HALLUIN was organised to cover a crossing of the river opposite RASCALS RETREAT.

A raft was constructed by the pioneers of the 1/4th Bn Cheshire Regt. and at 12.55 the first party of the 1/1st Bn Hereford Regt led by 2/Lt. Jenkins of the 1/4th Bn Cheshire Regt. crossed the river on the raft under cover of the artillery bombardment and lewis gun fire.

They succeeded in establishing themselves on the Southern bank of the river. As the raft only held two or three men it was 18.00 before the whole of "A" Coy. of the 1/1st Bn Hereford Regt. were ferried across and positions taken up along the railway in R.19.a.

The enemy soon opened out on this Company with 4.2's and minenwerfer and machine gun fire from ROOMY WOOD but though some casualties were sustained positions were maintained until dark and post handed over to 90th Bde. on relief.

Another attempt to cross at the LOCK failed owing to consistent shelling both with high explosive and gas of this vicinity.

Orders were received for the 102nd Inf. Bde. to be relieved by the 90th Bde. of the 30th Division.

The whole Brigade front was taken over by one battalion the 2nd/18th Bn of the London Regt. - relief commencing at 17.00.

their position The Company of the Scottish Rifles who had maintained South of the river opposite MARATHON BRIDGE during the whole day despite heavy hostile fire were withdrawn across the river at dusk from the Brigade front.

The relief by the 2/16th Bn. London Regt. was complete by 23.00, the delay being due to the necessity of relieving the only troops across the river - the Company at RASCALS RETREAT - by means of single raft.

On relief the whole Brigade was withdrawn to an area just North of GHELUWE where the Brigade became Divisional Reserve - Brigade Headquarters being established at JOHNSONS FARM - K.36.a.7.5. During the period from the morning of the 14th to the morning of the 17th the casualties suffered by the Brigade amounted to :-

KILLED		WOUNDED		MISSING	
Off.	O.Rs	Off.	O.Rs.	Off.	O.Rs.
4	44	10	198	-	47

and in addition approximately 3 Off. & 30 O.Rs were

OCT. 16th (continued).

evacuated as gas cases.

A large number of German dead were left on the field and it was found impossible to obtain a really accurate estimate of the material captured.

There was no hitch in the evacuation of the wounded.

Rations were delivered to Battalions each night and no difficulty was experienced in the supply of ammunition.

The supply of smoke bombs for the stokes mortars was very limited - only some 80 being available, - as all these had to be made by the T.M. Battery itself.

Great difficulty was experienced in maintaining an efficient telephone communication both forward and to the rear which was due to the length of communications and to the numerous exchanges through which every line was laid.

OCT. 17th.

The 102nd Inf. Bde. were held in readiness to move at 1 hours notice. All time was devoted to cleaning up and refitting of units.

OCT. 18th.

During the afternoon orders were received that the 34th Division would continue the advance - the 101st Inf. Bde. who were holding the line about WEVELGHEM forming the advance guard with the 102nd Inf. Bde. in support and the 103rd Inf. Bde. in reserve.

A warning order was issued to units to be ready to move at dawn and detailed orders were issued during the night.

OCT. 19th.

At 06.00 hours the 102nd Infantry Brigade Group composed of 102nd Infantry Brigade together with B Coy Machine Gun Battalion, 208th Field Coy. R.E. and C Coy Som L.I. moved by march route and were assembled by 09.00 with the heads of columns on the MENIN— EVELGHEM Road in squares R.10 and 11 by 09.00 awaiting orders to advance Brigade Headquarters was established at KRUISHOEK in close proximity to Advanced Divisional Headquarters.

As soon as all units were assembled orders are received to move the Brigade Group across the LYS. This was done by crossing the Pontoon Bridge in R.17.d. and the Brigade was halted in the area just west of LAUWE.

Brigade Headquarters moved from KRUISHOEK to a farm in R.17.d. where telephone communication as established with Division through 101st Inf. Bde. Headquarters who were in this vicinity. The move as completed by 10.00

7.

OCT. 19th (continued)

Dinners were taken as soon as ready. At 11.00 orders were issued for an immediate move to AELBEKE by the LAUWE—KNOCK Station – AELBEKE Road – where the Brigade was billetted by 16.00.

It was expected that the Brigade would remain at AELBEKE for the night but shortly after 16.00 orders were received to move at once to ST ANNE Area. This move was accomplished before dark – all units obtaining billets in the Convent at St. ANNE and the neighbouring Farms, where the Brigade remained for the night 19/20th after having marched 19 miles during the day.

OCT. 20th to OCT. 22nd

The Brigade remained at ST. ANNE ready to move at short notice.

Frequent reconnaissances were made to the forward area to enable units to keep in touch with progress of the advance and the routes to the front.

OCT. 22nd.

Orders were received that the 102nd Inf. Bde. would relieve the 124th Inf. Bde. of the 41st Division in the line.

OCT. 23rd.

The 102nd Infantry Brigade Group moved by march route at 09.40 via BELLEGHEM and ~~proceeded~~ bivouaced in the area just West of BELLEGHEM BOSCH with Brigade H.Q. in the Farm at U.1.b.8.4. arriving at noon. Parties were immediately sent forward to reconnoitre the line and orders were issued for as much of the relief as possible to be carried out before dark.

It was only found possible to relieve the supporting units by daylight, the remainder of relief being carried out after dark. The line taken over ran from the CANAL TUNNEL (held by the enemy) in O.22.d. ACHTERHOEK – BAVELHUMKNOK—POWDERIEGH all inclusive. The front was held by the 1/1st Bn. Hereford Regt. on the left and the 1/7th Bn Cheshire Regt. on the right with the inter-battalion boundary at U.8.a.central.

The 1/4th Bn Cheshire Regt. were in reserve at O.32.d. and U.2.b.

OCT. 24th.

During the night Brigade Order No. 215 was issued arranging for the co-operation of the 102nd Inf. Bde. with the attack of the 123rd Inf. Bde. East of the Canal.

In accordance with these orders the 1/1st Bn. Hereford Regt. moved their support and reserve Companies to within 500x of the crossing over the Canal Tunnel, with a view to following the right battalion of the 123rd Inf. Bde. as it attacked in a S.E. direction and filling the gap between their Brigade and the Canal.

2.

OCT. 24th (continued)

The remaining two Companies of the 1/1st Bn. Hereford Regt. were in readiness to form up, move from the original front line and follow their foremost Companies over the canal.

The 1/4th Bn Cheshire Regt. were ordered to move from their reserve position to the proximity of the Canal crossing as soon as this area was vacated by the 1/1st Bn. Hereford Regt.

Zero hour was at 0215 enabling battalions just sufficient time to make their dispositions.

At 02.15 the 1/1st Bn Hereford Regt reported considerable machine gun fire across the tunnel, from which it became evident that no progress had been made by the 183rd Infantry Brigade East of the Canal.

The 1/1st Bn Hereford Regt. remained in a position of readiness throughout the day to cross the tunnel should opportunity occur.

At 10.00 the Brigadier General Commanding was summoned to a conference at Divisional Headquarters.

On his return Officers Commanding Units were ordered to Brigade Headquarters and a scheme for advancing our line to the river SCHELDT both West and East of the COURTRAI---BOSSUYT-CANAL was outlined.

At 18.00 on the 24th the 1/4th Bn Cheshire Regt. was moved from its reserve position in O.33.a. across the COURTRAI---BOSSUYT CANAL by the KNOKKE Bridge and assembled in the area between the front line held by the 183rd Inf. Bde. in O.22.b. and the KNOKKE Bridge.

This assembly was completed by 23.30 on the 24th.

Detailed orders were received from Divisional Headquarters between 16.00 and 17.00 and during the night Brigade order No. 206 and instructions for the attack were issued.

OCT. 25th.

These were taken to the 1/4th Bn Cheshire Regt. and 1/1st Bn. Hereford Regt. by the Brigadier General Commanding at 02.00. and were sent by runner to the 1/7th Bn Cheshire Regt and remaining units.

At 03.00 25th in accordance with instructions issued the 1/7th Bn Cheshire Regt. endeavoured under an artillery barrage to effect crossings over the canal at Locks 3, 4 and 5. These attempts were frustrated by hostile machine guns, but the troops of this battalion remained in any forward position to which they had moved in close proximity to these locks to repeat this subsidiary operation in conjunction with the major operation at 09.04.

(Oct. 25th contd)

Shortly after this attempt a hostile counter attack developed against a company of the 1/7th Btn. Cheshire Regt. facing Lock 5, resulting in this post having to fall back about 200 yards and causing about 40 casualties (including Missing).

At 0902 the barrage of the 41st Division commenced EAST of the canal and as it crept forward the 1/4th Bn. Cheshire Regt. moved on the right of the 23rd Btn. Middlesex Regt. and as the right flank of this Battalion moved in a S.E. direction the 1/4th Batt. Cheshire Regiment extended its front to keep in touch, thus filling gap between Canal and the 23rd Btn. Middlesex Regt.

By approximately 0930 the 1/4th Bn. Cheshire Regt were clear of the Canal Tunnel and the 1/1st Bn. Hereford Regt. moved across the tunnel immediately in rear.

The advance was carried out with rapidity and with but slight opposition from the enemy.

What opposition was encountered came from the left flank where the advance of the 123rd Infantry Brigade failed to keep up with the barrage practically from the start of the operation.

At 1215 two companies of the 1/4th Bn. Cheshire Regt. were reported EAST of MOEN, one company SOUTH of MOEN, and one company WEST of the village along the canal.

The mopping up of the area had in the meantime been carried out by the 1/1st Bn. Hereford Regt., and about 13.00 two companies of this battalion entered MOEN and cleared the village, silencing and capturing two machine guns.

Attempts of the 1/7th Bn. Cheshire Regt. to force a crossing over the lock during the morning to harrass the enemy's withdrawal failed, but the capture of BOSSUYT and advance of an outpost line to the river was effected shortly after the main attack commenced.

By 1300 the Brigade on the left had entirely lost touch with the barrage and were reported to be held up by machine gun fire about HEESTERT.

Col. Drage, D.S.O., commanding the 1/4th Bn. Cheshire Regt. reformed and re-organised his battalion at 1300 SOUTH of MOEN and re-commenced the advance with the left of the Brigade on the MOEN-AUTRYVE ROAD and the right on the canal. To protect the left flank of the advance the 1/1st Bn. Hereford Regt. were ordered to form a defensive flank keeping touch with the right of the 41st Division.

OCT. 25th (continued)

About this time the 1/7th Bn Cheshire Regt. crossed the river at LOCK 5 and gaining touch with the 1/4th Bn Cheshire Regt. advanced along the EAST bank of the canal.

At 18.00 our troops were North of AUTRYVE and entered the village shortly afterwards when our guns had lifted off the village.

By 20.00 reports were received that all objectives had been reached.

The advance of the 1/4th Bn Cheshire Regt. was carried out with the loss of 2 officers wounded, 10 other ranks killed and 22 other ranks wounded. A total capture of 87 prisoners was reported.

The success was gained in spite of the fact that the 23rd Middlesex Regt. - the battalion operating on the left of the Brigade - was held up early in the day by machine gun fire causing the left flank of the Brigade to be greatly exposed, and by the evening of the 25th had only established themselves on a line P.28. P.32.central.

During the night Battalion fronts were re-adjusted. 24? The 1/7th Bn Cheshire Regt. held the line from U.34.central in touch with the 30th Division to BOSSUYT--MOEN Road and the 1/4th Bn. Cheshire Regt. continued the line to AUTRYBE, inclusive.

Posts were established along the Northern bank of the SCHELDT along the whole Brigade front. The 1/1st Bn Hereford Regt. were withdrawn to reserve and assembled S.E. of MOEN.

The night passed quietly except for hostile artillery and trench mortar activity which was chiefly confined to AUTRYVE-- MOEN and the wood in U.18.

A large number of civilians were released from enemy hands in BOSSUYT and AUTRYVE but great difficulty was experienced in getting them away owing to hostile shelling and gas.

Since the morning of the 20th the total casualties sustained by the Brigade amounted to 4 Officers and 85 O.R's. The prisoners reported as captured totalled 87 though this number was not reported as having past through the Divisional cage. 13 machine guns were among the material captured from the enemy.

The 26th passed quietly and the positions of the Brigade were further secured by the evacuation of AVELGHEM by the enemy and the consequent advance of the 41st Division during the morning.

The Brigade was relieved by the 21st Inf. Bde. of the 30th Division during the night 26/27th, relief being completed by 05.00 27th.

The Brigade on relief was concentrated in the area just East of HELLEGHEM BOSCH by 06.00.

The whole Brigade Group moved at 10.00 on the 27th to the ST.ANNE area arriving at midday.

Secret.   Copy No.

102nd INFANTRY BRIGADE ORDER No. 255

Reference map   2 : 10 : 1918.
Sheet 28 S.E. 1:20,000.

1.   Troops of the 35th and 41st Divisions are reported to be held up West of the GHELUWE SWITCH.

2.   102nd Infantry Brigade with 'D' Company Machine Gun Battalion will be prepared :-

   (a)   to take over a portion of the line now held by the 35th and 41st Divisions.

   (b)   to attack the GHELUWE SWITCH.

   In either event boundaries will be as follows :-

Northern Brigade boundary the YPRES--GHELUWE ROAD.
Southern Brigade boundary a North-West and South-East line running through Q.8., 15 and 22 central.

The inter-Battalion boundary approximately junction of roads at Q.3.c.6.0. - along road to junction of road and railway at Q.9.a.9.6. - thence a line running due South-East (this boundary must be arranged between Battalion Commanders concerned.)

3.   In either event the Brigade front will be taken over as follows :-

               1/4th Bn Cheshire Regt .. on the left
               1/7th Bn Cheshire Regt .. on the right
               1/1st Bn Hereford Regt .. in Support.

   O's. C. "D" Coy. M.G. Bn. and 102nd L.T.M.B. should reconnoitre positions to cover this front.

4.   103rd Infantry Brigade will be on the ~~left~~ RIGHT and the 41st Division on the LEFT.

5.   102nd Inf. Bde. Headquarters are remaining in present location, but in the event of the relief or operation mentioned above taking place, it will move to BLEGNAERT FME at P.12.c.1.9

6.   Acknowledge.

                                                        Captain.
                                                  BRIGADE MAJOR.
102 B.H.Q.   102nd INFANTRY BRIGADE.

               Copy No. 1 .. G.O.C.
                        2 .. 1/4th Bn Cheshire Regt.
                        3 .. 1/7th Bn Cheshire Regt.
                        4 ... 1/1st Bn Hereford Regt.
                        5 ... 102nd L.T.M.B.
                        6 ... "D" Coy. M.G. Bn.
                        7 ... O. C. 102 Bde. Signals.
                        8 ... War Diary.

SECRET
COPY No. 10.
5th Oct. 1918.

102nd Infantry Brigade Order No. 257.

Ref. Map Sh. 28 SE 1/20000.

1. (A) The Division will take up the front from KLIJTMOLEN Q 8. c. 5. 4. exclusive, to road junction K. 34. c. 9. 1. with the 102nd Inf. Bde. on the Right and the 101st Inf Bde. on the Left.

(B) Inter-brigade and inter-battalion boundaries will be as shown on map which will be issued separately to Units of the 102nd Inf Bde.

2. (A) The 1/7th Bn Cheshire Regt. will extend their Right and relieve troops of the 103rd Inf Bde. as far as KLIJTMOLEN Q.8.c.5.4 exclusive, as soon as possible after dusk tonight, Oct. 5/6th. Completion of relief will be reported by wire to this office by the code word "LEA".

(B) The 89th Inf. Bde of the 30th Division are relieving the 103rd

Sheet 2

Infantry Brigade from KLIJTMOLEN, inclusive, to the present Right boundary of the 103rd Inf Bde. tonight Oct. 5/6th. The 1/7th Bn Cheshire Regt will get into touch with troops of 89th Inf Bde and report by wire when this has been done.

(c) The 101st Inf Bde. are relieving the 124th Inf Bde. from the Left of the 1/4th Bn. Cheshire Regt to road junction K.34.c.9.1. tonight, Oct. 5/6th.

The 1/4th Bn Cheshire Regt will get into touch with Right of the 101st Inf Bde and report by wire when this has been done.

2. O.C. D Coy. M.G. Batt. will make arrangements to cover the extended Right Flank of the 102nd Inf Bde.

4 Bde. H.Q. will remain at BLEGNMERT FARM.

5 ACKNOWLEDGE. Done

358/6-40hrs

M Carr Captain.
Bde Major
102nd Inf Bde.

SECRET.

5th October 1918.

102ND INFANTRY BRIGADE ORDER NO. 257.

Reference Map Sheet 28 S.E. 1/20,000

1. (a) The Division will take up the Front from KLIJTMOLEN Q.8.c.5.4. exclusive to road junction K.34.c.9.1. with the 102nd Infantry Brigade on the Right and the 101st Infantry Brigade on the Left.

   (b) Inter-Brigade and Inter-Battalion boundaries will be as shown on map which will be issued separately to Units of the 102nd Infantry Brigade.

2. (a) The 1/7th Bn. Cheshire Regiment will extend their Right and relieve troops of the 103rd Infantry Brigade as far as KLIJTMOLEN Q.8.c.5.4. exclusive as soon as possible after dusk to-night October 5th.

   Completion of relief will be reported by wire to this Office by the code word "LEA".

   (b) The 89th Infantry Brigade of the 30th Division are relieving troops of the 103rd Infantry Brigade from KLIJTMOLEN inclusive to the present Right boundary of the 103rd Infantry Bde. to-night October 5th.
   The 1/7th Bn. Cheshire Regt will get into touch with troops of the 89th Infantry Brigade and report by wire when this has been done.

   (c) The 101st Infantry Brigade are relieving the 124th Infantry Brigade from the Left of the 1/4th Bn. Cheshire Regt to road junction K.34.c.9.1. to-night October 5/6th.
   The 1/4th Bn. Cheshire Regt will get into touch with Right of the 101st Infantry Brigade and report by wire when this has been done.

3. O.C. "D" Coy. M.G.Bn. will make arrangements to cover the extended Right flank of the 102nd Infantry Brigade.

4. Brigade Headquarters will remain at BLEGNAERT FARM.

5. ACKNOWLEDGE.

(sd) M. Carr
Captain,
Brigade Major,
102nd Infantry Brigade.

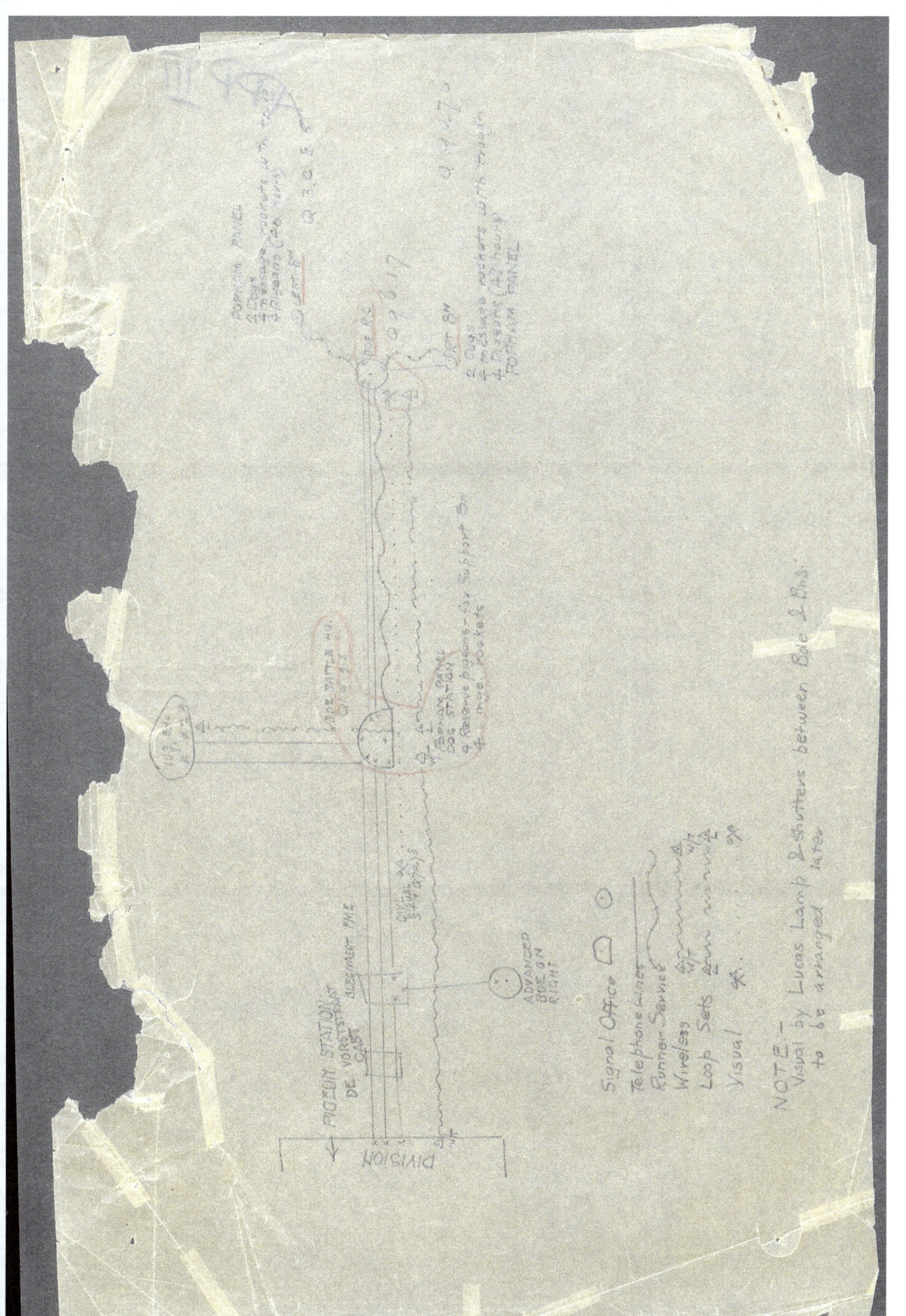

To _Bde Intelligence Off_ TS 66/32

    Herewith please find copy No..... of 102nd Infantry Brigade Instructions No. 1.

    Please acknowledge.

                                                          Captain,
                                                          Brigade Major,
../10/1918.   102nd Infantry Brigade.

SECRET.
Copy No..... 14

102ND INFANTRY BRIGADE INSTRUCTIONS NO. 1.
15th October 1918.

Reference Map. Sheet 28 S.E., 1/20,000.

1. The advance of the Second Army will be resumed on "J" day (not earlier than 14th October).

    The 34th Division will attack with the 30th Division on its Right and the 41st Division on its Left.

    The 102nd Infantry Brigade will be the Right and the 103rd Infantry Brigade the Left attacking Brigades of the 34th Division.

    The advance will be divided into three phases :-

    1st Phase to the BLACK LINE.
    2nd Phase to the BLUE LINE.
    3rd Phase to the final objective BROWN LINE.

    The objective lines, inter-divisional, inter-brigade and inter-battalion boundaries for the 102nd Infantry Brigade and the Infantry Starting Line, are shown on Map issued separately to Units of the 102nd Infantry Brigade.

PLAN OF ATTACK.

'A'. ARTILLERY.

2. **1st PHASE.**

    (a) The Infantry advance will commence at H hour. At H - 2 minutes the Field Artillery will put down a barrage on a line 200 yards in front of the Starting Line and will lift off that line at H plus 2 minutes.

    During the four minutes from H - 2 minutes to H plus two minutes the leading troops of assaulting Battalions will get as close as possible to the barrage.

    (b) The barrage will move forward at the rate of 100 yards in two minutes by lifts of 100 yards until it reaches a line 200 yards EAST of the BLACK LINE at H plus 28 minutes when it will halt for 15 minutes.

    (c) During this phase the Field Howitzers and Heavy Artillery will move ahead of the 18 pdr. barrage engaging all targets within their zones resting at the end of the phase on a line 800 yards EAST of the BLACK LINE and continuing to engage targets EAST of that Line.

3. **2nd PHASE.**

    (a) At the end of the 15 minutes pause (H plus 43 minutes) the creeping 18 pdr. barrage will move forward at the same rate as before until it reaches a line 250 yards EAST of the BLUE LINE at H plus 'a' minutes (a) where it will remain for 15 minutes.

    (b) The Field Howitzers and Heavy Artillery barrage will move forward as described in para. 2 (c) to 800 yards EAST of the BLUE LINE and in the case of the 102nd Infantry Brigade EAST of the BROWN LINE.

3. **3rd PHASE.**

    (a) At the end of the 15 minutes pause EAST of the 2nd Objective a proportion of the Field Artillery will form a protective barrage covering the Southern part of the objective which will have been reached by the 102nd Infantry Brigade and a portion of the 103rd Infantry Brigade during the 2nd phase.

Sheet 2.

A proportion of the Heavy Artillery will engage targets EAST of the Field Artillery barrage paying particular attention to the exits from MENIN.

(b) At H plus 'e' minutes the Field Artillery will cease fire.

(c) NOTE: THE EXACT TIMINGS OF THE ABOVE LIFTS ARE LIABLE TO CHANGE AND WILL THEREFORE BE NOTIFIED WHEN FINALLY SETTLED BY STATING THE VALUE TO BE ALLOTTED TO THE SMALL LETTERS QUOTED.

Copy No. 14
11th Octr. 1918.

ADDENDUM NO. 2 TO 102ND INFANTRY BRIGADE INSTRUCTIONS NO. 1.

1. The 1/8th Battalion Scottish Rifles of the 103rd Infantry Brigade will be operating on the Left of the 1/4th Bn. Cheshire Regiment.

M Carr
Captain,
Brigade Major,
102nd Infantry Brigade.

Sheet 3

"B". INFANTRY.

5. DISPOSITIONS FOR THE ATTACK.

(a)   The 102nd Infantry Brigade will attack with the 1/4th Batt. Cheshire Regiment on the Left and the 1/7th Batt. Cheshire Regiment on the Right.

Each Battalion will attack on a frontage of two Companies with one Company in Support and one Company in Reserve.

The 1/1st Batt. Hereford Regiment will be in Brigade Reserve.

All Units will be in their assembly positions with the leading troops on the Starting Line (as shown on Map) by H - 2 hours.

(b)   At this hour Battalions must be disposed in depth in their fighting formations, distance between echelons while in assembly positions being reduced as much as possible.

A report will be sent to Brigade Headquarters as soon as Battalions have completed assembly which must be finished by H - 2 hours.

(c)   The attack will be carried out in three phases as given below.

1st PHASE.

(a) (i) During the four minutes from H-2. to H plus 2 minutes the attacking companies will get as near as possible to the initial barrage line and advance as close as possible under the barrage to the 1st Objective where they will halt for 15 minutes - H plus 28 minutes to H plus 43 minutes.

(ii) During this pause troops must be re-organised into their proper formations. Troops detailed to clear defensive posts must rejoin their formations as soon as their task is completed.

(b) (i) No troops will advance under the barrage through GHELUVELT Village. The 103rd Infantry Brigade are detailing special troops to deal with the Village.
The Village will be smoked and engaged with Thermite Shell from H - 2 minutes till H plus 28 minutes by Special Company, R.E.

(ii) The leading troops of the 103rd Infantry Brigade will pass North and South of the Village, none being within 100 yards of the line on the Map marking the limits of the Village. To do this troops of the 103rd Infantry Brigade moving South of the Village will move in the area of the 1/4th Batt. Cheshire Regiment where necessary. As they clear the Village they will incline towards the MENIN ROAD EAST of the Village.

(iii) The troops of the 103rd Infantry Brigade detailed to deal with the Village will clear it from the North and South.

2nd PHASE

(a) The advance will be resumed at H plus 45 minutes the leading troops having previously closed up to the protective barrage line and will be continued to the 2nd Objective (BLUE LINE) as before.

(b) On the front of the 102nd Infantry Brigade and on the Right of the 103rd Infantry Brigade (i.e. from the Farm at Q.12.d.95.80 inclusive southwards to the MENIN ROAD) the 2nd Objective is the final objective. The barrage in front of this portion of the line will ~~stanceconsqmmences~~ remain 250 yards beyond it and troops as they arrive on the line will at once re-organise and consolidate the tactical points on the line.

(c) On the remainder of the front of the 103rd Infantry Brigade troops on reaching the 2nd Objective will re-organise and prepare for the advance to the final objective.

3rd PHASE.

(a) The 102nd Infantry Brigade will continue consolidati (on and re-organise.

(b) The 103rd Infantry Brigade will continue the advance pivoting on the Right about the Farm Q.12.d.95.80.

Sheet 5.

9. **ACTION FOR ASSAULTING COMPANIES.**

(a) (1) So far as can be ascertained the defence of the area to be attacked consists of fortified farms and pill boxes and these conditions probably exist in the trench system of the PORTION SECTOR. (Areas that are being engaged by Artillery are shown on the trading hassel separately) For this reason Battalions will advance in small groups and not in successive lines.

(b) The advance will be carried out under a creeping barrage and the leading troops will push straight on as close as possible to the barrage leaving defensive posts to be cleared by the mopping up parties. The two attacking companies will be strong companies and each platoon of each Company must have its allotted objective details in order.

(c) The whole attacking force must get right up to the initial barrage and keep up to it going straight through to each objective.

Commanding Officers are reminded that the barrage is fast and all ranks should be specially warned of this fact.

(d) Special emphasis is to be laid on the method of advance in small groups - small columns or sections in single file. The advance of one column must not be stopped because the columns on its flank are held up.

The principle of pushing on where resistance is least instead of reinforcing held up troops must invariably be observed unless casualties are so great as to necessitate reinforcement.

The pushing forward of parties where resistance is least facilitates the advance of parties that are held up.

(e) Full use must be made of smoke rifle grenades by the leading troops to mask the defensive hostile posts.

10. **DETAILS OF MOPPING UP STRONG POSITIONS.**

(a) Battalion Commanders will detail special parties (platoons or stronger as may be thought necessary) to mop up known pill boxes or strong points. These parties will be detailed from the Support and Reserve Companies of the battalion.

Orders issued by the Officers Commanding Battalions will specify which platoon is to deal with which defensive post naming the O.C. and NO. of the platoon.

(b) The Support and Reserve Companies will have special objectives allotted to them in each phase.

All parties detailed for mopping up will rejoin their company immediately their task is completed.

11. **LIAISON.**

(a) Throughout the advance the closest liaison must be kept up by specially detailed parties in all echelons.

(b) The 1/7th Bn. Cheshire Regiment will detail a special liaison patrol to keep touch with the 36th Division on its right and will take special measures to protect

its flank............

Sheet 4.

its flank should the advance of the Division on the Right be held up.

The 1/4th Btn. Cheshire Regiment will carry out the same procedure with the 103rd Infantry Brigade.

(c) Each attacking battalion will detail a liaison patrol to keep touch on the inner flanks of Battalions. These parties to be specially detailed and named.

12. GUIDES.

(a) Battalion Commanders are reminded that the advance is in a S.E. direction and that the keeping of direction is of the utmost importance.

(b) Specially selected guides must be detailed to each Company to ensure that direction is kept. The advance is not a long one, and no difficulty should be experienced in selecting prominent points to move on.

13. RE-ORGANISATION AND CONSOLIDATION.

(a) Battalion Commanders must endeavour to arrive at the final objective with sufficient troops to overcome any opposition.

(b) Battalion and Company Commanders must re-organise their units as quickly as possible during each phase to be ready to move forward again.

(c) Immediately the final objective is gained it will be consolidated.
Battalion Commanders must realise that the coloured lines are only approximate and that they must decide their line - especially the BROWN LINE according to the nature of the ground.

(d) In addition to the consolidation of the final objective (BROWN LINE) the line shown on the map in YELLOW is also to be consolidated as a support line of strong points.
This task may be carried out by the moving up of the 1/1st 5th Hereford Regiment or by thinning out troops of the attacking Battalions.

14. EXPLOITATION.

(a) The protective barrage will lift off the whole of the front at H plus 'e' minutes.
Patrols must be pushed out as far as possible under the protective barrage and seize and occupy any strong point or pill box, and at H plus 'e' minutes strong patrols will push forward at least to the line WERVICQ - MENIN RAILWAY and the western exits of MENIN.

15. ASSEMBLY.

(a) When the Battalions move up to the line at least 24 hours previous to H hour, they will take over the line in fighting formation - the two attacking Companies in the front line and the Support and Reserve Companies in their respective places, and during the day previous to J day all Company and platoon Officers must instruct their N.C.Os, and men as much

as possible...........

sheet 7.

as possible.

15. (b) The 1/1st Btn Hereford Regiment will take up its position disposed in depth with two Companies in front, one in Support and one in Reserve. It will probably not move from Divisional Reserve area until J minus 1/J night.

The Battalion may move forward to consolidate the YELLOW LINE during J day or on J/J plus 1 night, but will not move without orders from Brigade Headquarters.

16. HEADQUARTERS.

At H hour Headquarters will be as shown in Appendix "A"

17. Every detail will be arranged before taking over the line. A copy of Battalion Orders will reach Brigade Headquarters not later than noon on the 12th instant with a rough map showing dispositions.

18. C. TRENCH MORTARS.

(a) The Officer Commanding 102nd. L.T.M.B. will detail two Stokes Mortars and teams to be attached to each attacking Battalion.

The remaining four guns will be attached to the Reserve Battalion, the 1/1st Btn Hereford Regiment.

(b) The 1/1st Btn Hereford Regiment will detail a carrying party of 1 N.C.O. and 5 men for each gun with attacking Battalions.

O.C. 102nd L.T.M.B. will notify O.C. 1/1st Btn. Hereford Regiment as to when and where he will require these parties.

(c) It is hoped that a supply of special smoke bombs will be available for use with Trench Mortars.

19. D. R.A.F.

(a) A contact patrol aeroplane of the 53rd Squadron R.A.F. will fly over the line to call for flares and discs at H plus 1 hour and H plus 2 hours and at such times as may be required.

All troops will be prepared to answer the call and to show their positions where called for.

This plane will be marked with two black rectangular flaps attached to or projecting from the lower plane on each side of the fuselage and a trailing streamer on the rudder.

(b) Two artillery machines and a counter-attack patrol will be out from dawn onwards.

(c) The squadron will be prepared to drop ammunition as asked for by Battalions with a "V" panel.

So far as the 102nd Infantry Brigade is concerned the most suitable place would be the vicinity of QUANDARY FARM (Q.17.b.1.8.)

(d) The squadron will also be prepared to drop pigeons if asked for by Battalions. The signal for the purpose will be four panels placed in a rectangle.

Captain.
Brigade Major.
102nd. Infantry Brigade.

APPENDIX "A"

Advanced Hd. Qrs. 54th Division..................O.8.c.7.8. (Sheet 28)

102nd Infantry Brigade Head Qrs.................Q.1.d.9.3.

1/4th Btn Cheshire Regt.........................Q.3.c.8.5.

1/7th Btn Cheshire Regt.........................Q.9.a.7.8.

1/1st Btn Hereford Regt.........................Q.2.c.5.8.8.

102nd L.T.M.B...................................Q.1.d.9.3.

103rd Infantry Brigade..........................K.31.c.9.9. (Sheet 28)

102nd. INFANTRY BRIGADE INSTRUCTIONS　　　　　SECRET.
　　　　　　　　NUMBER 2.　　　　　　　　　　　　Copy No. 14

　　　　　　　　　　　　　　　　　　　　　　　11th October 1918.

Reference Map Sheet 28. 1/40,000.

'E'. MACHINE GUNS.

1. (a). 'A' Company, 34th Battalion Machine Gun Corps will be attached to the 102nd Infantry Brigade from H - 2 onwards.

   (b). 4 guns will be attached to each Battalion. The remaining 4 guns will be held in Brigade Reserve.

   (c). Guns attached to attacking Battalions should be used well forward. They should not be moved unless absolutely necessary until the final objective is captured. Battalion Commanders are reminded that it is better to inform Machine Gun Commanders where the fire of Machine Guns is required rather than to direct the guns to be placed in certain places.

'F'. R.E., and PIONEERS.

2. (a). 'B' Section, No. 4 Special Company, R.E. has been placed at the disposal of the Division for the purpose of smoking GHELUWE Village.

   (b). It will take up the positions for two groups of approximately 3 mortars each at about Q.3.b.8.4. and Q.3.d.95.30.

   (c). The mortars have a range of 900 yards and will fire smoke on the North West and South faces of GHELUWE Village, from H - 2 minutes to about H plus 8 minutes and Thermite from about H plus 8 minutes to H plus 28 minutes and then cease fire.
   The exact time of changing from smoke to thermite depends on the strength and direction of the wind and will be settled by the Officer Commanding at the time.
   If the wind is anywhere EAST of S.S.W. and N.N.W. both inclusive, the G.O.R.A. will arrange for Field Howitzers to assist in smoking the EASTERN edge of the Village.

   (d). One Section of Field Company, R.E., and half a Pioneer Company have been placed at the disposal of the 102nd Infantry Brigade to assist in consolidation.
   Further orders will be issued as to their employment.

　　　　　　　　　　　　　　　　　　　　Captain,
　　　　　　　　　　　　　　　　　　　　Brigade Major,
　　　　　　　　　　　　　　　　　　　102nd Infantry Brigade.

Issued to all recipients of 102nd Infantry Brigade Instructions No. 1 dated 10/10/1918.

ADDENDUM NO. 1 to 102nd. INFANTRY BRIGADE
INSTRUCTIONS NO. 1.

Copy No 14

11th October 1918.

1. **LIAISON.**

The 1/7th Btn Cheshire Regiment will establish liaison posts with the 30th Division on the Right at PRICELESS HOUSE Q.16.a., and at Cross Roads Q.17.c.2.2. The establishment of these posts will be reported to Brigade Headquarters.

2. **ARTILLERY.**

(a) The 102nd Infantry Brigade will be supported by the 152nd. Brigade R.F.A., and a portion of the 96th Army F.A. Brigade and a considerable amount of heavy artillery. The 152nd. Brigade R.F.A., will probably move forward such batteries as are necessary to cover the Line of the WERVICQ - MENIN Railway and as far EAST as possible after the capture of the final objective.

(b) There will be a bombardment with B.B. shell by Xth Corps heavy artillery on the night of J - 1/J.
ZERO hour will be 19.00.
The Xth Corps is bombarding the EASTERN portion of W.2 with special attention to O.P's.

3. **ASSEMBLY.**

The C.R.E. is marking out with Green Sign Posts a combined Infantry and Bundle path as follows:-

HOLLEBEKE CHATEAU - DEVOKSTSTRAAT CABT. - P.4.a. -
NEW GERMAN ROAD just N. of Farm of GROS BALLOT - P.5.a.

This will be referred to in future as 'THE GREEN TRACK'

All Units will reconnoitre the track.

4. **INTELLIGENCE.**

One platoon of 'C' Company, Xth Corps Cyclist Battalion will be attached to the 102nd. Infantry Brigade.

It is probably that at least one section will be attached to each attacking Battalion for special patrol work - not for message carrying - as the fight develops.

Captain.
Brigade Major.
102nd Infantry Brigade.

Issued to all recipients of 102nd Infantry Brigade Instructions No. 1 dated 10/10/1918.

Identification Trace for use with Artillery Maps.

Secret.

Trace A1 to accompany M.I.A.
showing Targets referred to in
Para 6 of Operation Instructions No 1
of 10.10.18

To Superimpose Sheet 28 SE
Scale 1/20000

SECRET.
Copy No. 64

102nd. INFANTRY BRIGADE INSTRUCTIONS NO. 2.

11th October 1918.

"A" COMMUNICATIONS.

1. (a) The main axis of communications will be advanced Divisional Headquarters, EVONS-KIRAAT CAMP – BLEUBARD FARM – SHEET FARM, C.7.a.7.0. – PILLBOX C.8.b.1.7.

    (b) A central visual station will be established from at C.7.a.7.0. for receiving M.L. messages from all stations on the Divisional Front.

    (c) Asstst receiving stations will be established at Advanced Brigade Headquarters and the Brigade Report Centre.

2. (a) All means of communication and the allotment of dogs pigeons, etc., to Units are shown on tracing attached. Battalions will ensure that all Battalion Signalling Stores are up to establishment and that all special stores issued are taken forward.

    (b) Attention is drawn to General Staff Instructions No 11, issued to Battalions of the 102nd Infantry Brigade under this Office letter No. F.S.66/60 dated 6-10-1918, the principles of which will be strictly adhered to.

                                        Captain.
                                        Brigade Major.
                                        102nd Infantry Brigade.

Issued to all recipients of 102nd Infantry Brigade
Instructions No 1 dated 10/10/1918.

SECRET.
Copy No...

102ND INFANTRY BRIGADE ORDER NO. 250
11th October 1918.

Reference Map.
Sheet 28 S.E. 1/20,000.

1. The 34th Division will resume the advance at H hour on J day.
   The 102nd Infantry Brigade will be the Right attacking Brigade
   Objectives, Boundaries, Plan of Attack, &c., for the 102nd
   Infantry Brigade have been laid down in Instructions issued to
   all concerned.

2. (a). The 102nd Infantry Brigade will relieve troops of the 101st
   Infantry Brigade from PILLBOX Q.10.a.22.70 inclusive to Q.9.c.0.5.
   on the night 12/13th October.

   (b) The 1/4th Battalion Cheshire Regiment will take over the Left
   Sector, and the 1/7th Bn. Cheshire Regiment the Right Sector of the
   Brigade Front, moving from present locations as soon as possible
   after dusk, relieving the 4th Bn. Royal Sussex Regiment and two
   Companies 2/4th Bn. Queens Regiment.
   Trench Mortars will be attached to Battalions in accordance
   with Instructions already issued.
   Brigade and inter-battalion boundaries are shown on map issued
   with Brigade Instructions No. 1.
   All details will be arranged between Commanding Officers
   concerned.
   The usual advance parties will proceed to the line on the
   11th instant, and will take over all stores, sector maps, &c.,
   from outgoing units.

3. The 1/1st Battalion Hereford Regiment will remain in its
   present area until dusk night 13/14th, when it will move to
   Brigade Reserve and take up positions about Q.2.c. as when last
   in the line.

4. Front Line Battalions will take over the line in their fighting
   formations with their two attacking Companies in the Front Line
   and the Support and Reserve Companies in their respective positions.
   The 1/1st Bn. Hereford Regiment will be disposed in depth with
   two Companies in Front, one in Support, and one in Reserve.

5. The 103rd Infantry Brigade will be on the left of the 102nd
   Infantry Brigade and the 90th Infantry Brigade on its Right.
   Touch must be established with flank Brigades.
   "A" Company, 34th M.G.Batt. are in the line covering the
   Brigade Front.

6. On the night J - 1/J the 2/4th Batt. Cheshire Regiment will
   straighten their line so that the Front Line of Posts will run
   from Q.10.a.0.5. Northwards along the North and South grid line
   between Q.9. and Q.10. This will be carried in conjunction with
   the 103rd Infantry Brigade who are executing a similar movement
   along the grid line to the MENIN ROAD, at Q.4.c.00.95. This
   movement will be completed by H - 3 hours.
   Completion of this move will be reported to Brigade Hd. Qrs.
   by the code word "SPILL".

7. Officers Commanding Battalions, T.M.B., and "A" Company, M.G.
   Battalion will send an Officer representative with three watches
   to Brigade Battle Headquarters, Q.1.d.9.3., by 17.00 hours J-day
   to synchronise watches.

8. The Staff Captain will issue instructions as to administrative
   arrangements for the relief and forthcoming operation.

9. Completion of relief will be reported to Brigade Hd. Qrs. by
   wire by code word "ORDER".
   The Command of Sector will pass to G.O.C. 102nd Infantry
   Brigade on completion of relief.

Sheet. 2.

10.   Brigade Headquarters will close at O.6.b.9.9. on the 12th instant and re-open at DEVORSTSTRAAT CABT. at an hour to be notified later.
        Brigade Headquarters, DEVORSTSTRAAT CABT. *will march from* and re-open at Battle Headquarters, Q.1.d.9.3. on J - 1 day at an hour to be notified later.

11.   The exact time and date of H hour and J day will be notified later.

12.   ACKNOWLEDGE.

                                    Captain,
                                Brigade Major,
                            102nd Infantry Brigade.

Issued to all recipients of 102nd Infantry Brigade Instructions No. 1 dated 10/10/1918.

SECRET.
COPY No. ...

13th October, 1918.

102ND INFANTRY BRIGADE INSTRUCTIONS NO. 4.

1. The general situation is such that the enemy may be contemplating a retreat from LILLE. Patrols must therefore be used boldly at night and touch kept with the enemy. Any retreat must be followed up.

2. The result of the operations on J day may hasten the enemy's retirement. If therefore the operations are successful the 30th Division on our Right will be ordered to push forward on both sides of WERVICQ on the evening of J day or J/J plus 1 night.

3. If the 30th Division pushed forward the right of the 34th Division will be ordered to cover the left of the 30th Division by advancing the line of the Right Brigade to the general line - Road in Q.35.central - GODOCS - QUERRY FARM - maintaining touch with the left of the 30th Division about the first named point.

M Carr
Captain,
Brigade Major,
102nd Infantry Brigade.

Issued to all recipients of 102nd Infantry Brigade Instruction
No. 1.

G.S.604   SECRET
           Copy No. 8
           14th Oct.1918

102nd Infantry Brigade Order no. 260.

Ref. map Sh. 28 S.E. 1/10000.

1. The 102nd Inf. Bde. will consolidate tonight the positions won today, forming a main line of resistance on the final objective, BROWN LINE, and a support line along the YELLOW LINE.

2. The 1/4th Bn. Cheshire Regt will consolidate the Left Sector from the MENIN road, inclusive, at Q.12.d.7.3 to Q.17.B.9.1. exclusive, and the 1/7th Bn. Cheshire Regt from Q.17.B.9.1. inclusive, to Cross Roads Q.17.c.2.2.

   Battalions will be disposed in depth and the 4 machine guns and 2 trench mortars attached to each Battalion will be placed in positions to cover the Front Line in case of counter attack.

   One Coy. of the 1/1st Bn. Hereford Regt will remain attached to the

Sheet 2

1/4th Bn Cheshire Regt.

3. 3 Coys of the 1/1st Bn Hereford Regt. will consolidate the YELLOW LINE within the Brigade boundaries, also disposed in depth.

4. 2 Coys. of the Batt. of the 101st Inf. Bde. are moving up to occupy the original front line. The Coy. of the 1/1st Bn Hereford Regt. at present in the original front line will not move to the YELLOW LINE until the above Coys. have arrived.

5. Patrols will be pushed out by front line Batts. to keep touch with the enemy and advanced posts will be established to secure the Western exits of MENIN. Should MENIN be found unoccupied patrols must be pushed through to secure river crossings South of the Town between RASCALS RETREAT and MARATHAN BRIDGE.

Sheet 3.

6. The 1/4th Bn. Cheshire Regt will establish a liaison post with the 103rd Inf. Bde. at Q.12.d.7.3. and the 1/7th Bn. Cheshire Regt a liaison post with the 90th Inf Bde at Q.17.c.2.2.
A liaison post between the 1/4th and 1/7th Bns Cheshire Regt will be formed at Q.17.B.9.1.
The 1/1st Bn. Hertford Regt will also establish liaison posts with flank Brigades on the YELLOW LINE.
The establishing of these posts will be reported by wire to Brigade H.Q.

7. The artillery S.O.S. lines will be on the WERVICQ - MENIN Railway.
O.C. Batts will keep Bde H.Q. informed of the progress of patrols and of the exact location of any post established forward of the BROWN LINE to enable the necessary adjustments to be made in the S.O.S. lines.

Sheet 4

8. The contact aeroplane will fly over the line tomorrow as soon as it is light enough to see. Front line troops will be ordered to do everything possible to reveal their position by lighting flares, flashing discs, waving, &c and orders to clear up the situation without fail.

9. Acknowledge by wire. Done Report dispositions as soon as possible tomorrow 15th inst.

M Carr Captain
Brigade Major
102nd Inf Bde

Copies to :-
3 3 Battalions
4 102 LTMB
5 A Coy 34 M G Bn
6 103rd Inf Bde
7 34 Div G
8 90 Inf Bde

SECRET.
14th October 1918.

APP. V

102ND INFANTRY BRIGADE ORDER NO. 260.

Reference Map. Sheet 28S.E./ 1/10,000
---

1. The 102nd Infantry Brigade will consolidate to-night the positions won to-day forming a main line of resistance on the final objective, BROWN LINE, and a support line along the YELLOW LINE.

2. The 1/4th Batt. Cheshire Regiment will consolidate the Left Sector from the MENIN road inclusive at Q.12.d.7.3. and the 1/7th Batt. Cheshire Regiment from Q.17.b.9.1. inclusive to Cross roads Q.17.c.2.2.
   Battalions will be disposed in depth and the 4 machine guns and 2 trench mortars attached to each Battalion will be placed at the disposal in positions to cover the Front Line in case of counter attack.
   One company of the 1/1st Batt. Hereford Regiment will remain attached to the 1/4th Bn. Cheshire Regiment.

3. 3 Companies of the 1/1st Battalion Hereford Regiment will consolidate the YELLOW LINE within the Brigade boundaries also disposed in depth.

4. 2 Companies of the Battalion of the 101st Infantry Brigade are moving up to occupy the original front line. The Company of the 1/1st Bn. Hereford Regiment at present in the original front line will not move to the YELLOW LINE until the above Companies have arrived.

5. Patrols will be pushed out by front line Battalions to keep touch with the enemy and advanced posts will be established to secure the Western exits of MENIN. Should MENIN be found unoccupied patrols must be pushed through to secure the river crossings South of the town between RASCALS RETREAT and MARATHON BRIDGE.

6. The 1/4th Bn. Cheshire Regiment will establish a liaison post with the 103rd Infantry Brigade at Q.12.d.7.3. and the 1/7th Bn. Cheshire Regiment a liaison post with the 90th Infantry Brigade at Q.17.c.2.2.
   A liaison post between the 1/4th Bn. Cheshire Regiment and the 1/7th Bn. Cheshire Regiment will be formed at Q.17.b.9.1.
   The 1/1st Battalion Hereford Regiment will also establish liaison posts with flank Brigades in the YELLOW LINE.
   The establishment of these posts will be reported to Brigade Headquarters.

7. The artillery S.O.S. lines will be on the WERVICQ - MENIN railway.
   O's.C. Battalions will keep Brigade Headquarters informed of the progress of patrols and of the exact location of any post established forward of the BROWN LINE to enable the necessary adjustments to be made in the S.O.S. lines.

8. The contact aeroplane will fly over the line to-morrow as soon as it is light enough to see. Front line troops will be warned to do everything possible to reveal their positions by lighting flares, flashing discs, waving, &c., in order to clear up the situation without fail.

9. Acknowledge by wire. Report dispositions as soon as possible to-morrow, 15th instant.

(Sgd) McCan,
Captain
Bde Major
102nd Inf Bde

SECRET   15-10-18

102nd Infantry Brigade Order No 261.

Ref. Map Sheet 28 SE 1/20000.

1. The new inter-brigade boundary will run as follows:—
GROUP FARMS – JOB FARM – BRIDGE OF ASSES (all inclusive) – thence along stream round Northern edge of MENIN to bend in river at R.14.b.8.6. – MARATHAN BRIDGE (inclusive to Right Brigade).

2. The 5th A.S.H. of the 103rd Inf. Bde. will take over the Front line from MARATHAN BRIDGE (exclusive) along LIVER LANE to TINT FARM relieving the 2 coys. of the 1/4th Bn. Cheshire Regt. to CIPLE TRACK and any troops of the 102nd Inf. Bde EAST of the new boundary.

3. The 1/1st Bn. Hereford Regt. will take over the present front of the 102nd Inf. Bde from the MARATHAN BRIDGE (inclusive) to MONGREL BRIDGE R.19.a (inclusive).

Sheet 2

getting into touch with troops of the 90th
Inf. Bde. on the Right who are reported
to be pushing up to the RIVER LYS
about MONGREL BRIDGE.

4. The 3 Coys. of the 1/1st Bn Hereford
Regt. at present holding the Brigade
Front under command of Lieut. Col.
Drage D.S.O. will remain in their
present positions disposed about
MARATHAN BRIDGE, THE LOCK and
MONGREL BRIDGE. All troops will
be NORTH or WEST of the River LYS
The remaining Company of the 1/1st
Bn Hereford Regt. will move up to
a support position relieving 2
Coys. of 1/4th Bn Cheshire Regt.
about Q 18 b and north of RATHO
JUNCTION. The H.Q. of the 1/1st
Bn Hereford Regt. will remain
at QUERY FARM or move forward
to the present H.Q. of the 1/4th
Bn Cheshire Regt as desired by
the Officer commanding concerned.

5. The 1/4th Bn Cheshire Regt. on
relief by the 103rd Inf Bde. and

Sheet 3

1/1st Bn Hereford Regt will withdraw to positions – to be selected by the Officer Commanding – WEST of the 1/7th Bn Cheshire Regt who have 3 Coys on the BROWN LINE from Q17 c 6.4. to Q12 d 6.8. and one Coy. in support at Q17 a 5.6. Troops will be disposed so as to cover the new Brigade Front, dispositions and location of Batt. H.Q. to be reported as soon as possible. Batt. will be in Bde. Reserve.

6. Command of the Front Line will pass to the Officer Commanding 1/1st Bn Hereford Regt on completion of relief.

The Officer Commanding 1/1st Bn Hereford Regt will as far as possible dispose his Batt. in depth.

7. The 1/7th Bn Cheshire Regt will remain in their present location but will extend their front to the BRIDGE OF ASSES exclusive.

Sheet 4

8. Completion of relief to be reported by code word MUG by wire.

9. ACKNOWLEDGE

M Carr Captain
Brigade Major
102nd Inf Bde

APP IV

SECRET

15th Oct. 1918.

102ND INFANTRY BRIGADE ORDER NO. 261.a.

Reference Map Sheet 28 S.E. 1/20,000.

1. The new inter-brigade boundary will run as follows:-

   GROUP FARMS - JOB FARM - BRIDGE OF ASSES (all inclusive) - thence along stream round Northern edge of MENIN to bend in river at R.14.b.8.6. - MARATHON BRIDGE (inclusive to Right Brigade.

2. The 5th A. & S. H. of the 103rd Infantry Brigade will take over the front line from MARATHON BRIDGE (exclusive) along LIVER LANE to TINT FARM relieving the two companies of the 1/4th Bn. Cheshire Regiment to CYPLE TRACK and any troops of the 102nd Infantry Brigade EAST of the new boundary.

3. The 1/1st Batt. Hereford Regt. will take over the present front of the 102nd Infantry Brigade from the MARATHON BRIDGE (inclusive) to MONGREL BRIDGE R.19.a. (inclusive), getting into touch with troops of the 90th Infantry Brigade on the Right who are reported to be pushing up to the RIVER LYS about MONGREL BRIDGE.

4. The 3 companies of the 1/1st Batt. Hereford Regiment at present holding the Brigade Front under command of Lieut. Col. DRAGE, D.S.O., will remain in their present positions disposed about MARATHON BRIDGE. All troops will be North and or West of the River LYS.

   The remaining Company of the 1/1st Bn. Hereford Regt. will move up to a support position relieving 2 Companies of 1/4th Bn. Cheshire Regiment about Q.18.b. and North of RATHO JUNCTION. The Headquarters of the 1/1stBn. Hereford Regiment will remain at QUERY FARM or move forward to the present Headquarters of the 1/4th Bn. Cheshire Regiment as desired by the Officer Commanding concerned.

5. The 1/4th Bn. Cheshire Regiment on relief by the 103rd Infantry Brigade and 1/1st Bn. Hereford Regt. will withdraw to positions - to be selected by the Officer Commanding - WEST of the 1/7th Bn. Cheshire Regt., who have 3 Companies on the BROWN LINE from Q.17.c.6.4. to Q.12.d.6.8. and one company in support at Q.17.a.5.6. Troops will be disposed so as to cover the new Brigade Front, dispositions and location of Battalion Headquarters to be reported as soon as possible. Battalions will be in Brigade Reserve.

6. Command of the front line will pass to the Officer Commanding 1/1st Bn. Hereford Regiment on completion of relief.
   The Officer Commanding 1/1st Bn. Hereford Regiment will as far as possible dispose his Battalion in depth.

7. The 1/7th Bn. Cheshire Regt will remain in their present location but will extend their front to the BRIDGE OF ASSES exclusive.

8. Completion of relief will be reported by code word "MUG" by wire.

9. ACKNOWLEDGE.

(sd) M. CARR,
Captain,
Brigade Major,
102nd Infantry Brigade.

SECRET

102nd Infantry Brigade
WARNING ORDER   G.S.616

Ref Map Sh 28 1/40000.

1. The 102nd Inf Bde. will be relieved by the 90th Inf. Bde. on the night 16th/17th.

2. On relief 102nd Inf Bde will move to area in K 35 and K 36 with Bde H.Q at JOHNSTONS FARM. K 36 a 7. 2.

3. The usual advance parties will meet the Staff Captain at JOHNSTONS FARM K 36 a 7. 2.:
   1 Officer & 1 runner per Batt H.Q;
   1 Officer, 1 N.C.O and 1 runner per Coy.
   1 Runner per platoon.
   at 10 am tomorrow 16th inst.

4. Detailed orders will be issued later.

5. ACKNOWLEDGE

                                Captain
                                Bde Major
15/10/18.   102nd Inf Bde.

SECRET.
Copy No. _____

19th October 1918.

102ND INFANTRY BRIGADE ORDER NO. 231.

Reference Map 1/40,000 Sheets 28 and 29.

1. (a) The Division will continue advance to-day starting at 0850.

    First Objective : ROLLEGHEM (excl) - ROLLEGHEMINOK N.20.b. (incl).

    If situation allows, Second Onjective will be :- T.3.a.5.8.- BELLEGHEM - ROLLEGHEMINOK.

    (b) 30th Division on Right - First Objective :- LE COMPAS (S.18.a.)- ROLLEGHEM (incl).
        Second Objective :- TOMBROEK - KALVERSTEERT - T.3.a.5.8.

    (c) 35th Division on Left :- First Objective - Road N.15.a. through POTTELBERG to COUTRAI.
        Second Objective :- N.20.b. to WALLE.

    (d) 35th Division advance commences at dawn.

    (e) Advance will be made irrespective of whether Divisions on flanks make progress, and dispositions are to be made to protect flanks accordingly.

2. 101st Infantry Brigade will form the advance guard. The 102nd Infantry Brigade will be in Support and the 103rd Infantry Brigade in Divisional Reserve.

3. The 102nd Infantry Brigade, consisting of Units as under, will move to a position of readiness with heads of Battalion Columns on the MENIN - WEVELGHEM Road in Squares R.10. 11. by 0930, 19th instant, inaccordance with Table "A" attached :-

    102nd Infantry Brigade.
    1 Company, 34th M.G. Corps.
    208th Field Company, R.E.
    1 Company, 2/4th Som. L.I. (Pioneers).

4. Battalions will move in Fighting Order and complete with Transport.
    The following intervals will be maintained on the line of march:-
        100 yards between Battalions.
        100 yards between Companies.
        25 yards between every six vehicles.
        100 yards between Unit and its Transport.

5. Units will report arrival to Brigade Hd. Qrs. by mounted orderly who will remain attached to Brigade Hd. Qrs. during the operations.

6. On arrival O.C., 102nd L.T.M.B. will despatch two Stokes Mortars and Teams to be attached to each Battn. The remaining Mortars will remain in Reserve.

7. Staff Captain will issue instructions as to administrative arrangements. All surplus stores will be dumped at JOHNSTONS FARM, K.36.a.7.2. before departure of Unit.

8. Brigade Hd.Qrs. will close at K.36.a.7.2. at 0715 and re-open at KRUISHOEK Fm. R.5.c. central at 0900.

9. ACKNOWLEDGE.

                                    Captain,
                                    Brigade Major,
                                    102nd Infantry Brigade.

TABLE "A"

Starting Point K.35.b.3.3. (Sheet 28)

Ser. No.	Unit.	From	To	Time head of Units Col. passes Starting Point.	Route	Remarks.
1.	1/1st Bn.Hereford Rgt.	K.35.b.	Road running from R.11.a.0.8. with head of Col. at x rds. R.11.c.3.5	0650	"A"	Units will assemble on either side of road given Transport will remain on road. Battalion or Units Hd. Qrs. will be at head of Column.
2.	1/7th Bn.Cheshire Rgt.	K.35.a.	Road running from R.10.b.1.2. with head of Col. R.10.d.5.4.	0705	"A"	
3.	1/4th Bn.Cheshire Rgt.	K.30.c.	Rd. running from R.10.a.2.1. with head of Col. at R.10.c.5.1.	0720	"B"	
4.	M.G.Coy.	GHELUWE	Rd. running from L.10.b.7.7. with head of Col. at R.10.b.1.2.	0735	"A"	
5.	102nd B.H.Q. 102nd L.T.M.B.	K.35.a.7.2.	KRUTSHOEK Fm. R.5.c.central	0740	"A"	
6.	208 Fd.Co. R.E.	GHELUWE	Rd. running from R.10.a.0.2. with hd. of col. at R.10.a.2.1.	0745	"B"	
7.	Coy. Bom. L.I.	Q.3.a.7.7.	--do--	0750	"B"	

ROUTE "A" : K.36.b.6.3.—L.25.d.8.5.—L.32.c.0.8.—L.32.b.C.2.—L.33.b.C.3.—L.34.d.6.3.—R.4.a.2.9.—L.34.d.8.2—Fm.L.4.b.7.0.— L.4.d.6.7. to R.11.a. and R.10.d.

ROUTE "B" : K.35.b.8.5.—L.25.d.8.3.—R.2.a.3.1.—R.2.b.5.4. (Rd.not shown on Map)—R.6.a.3.2.—R.9.a.3.8.—R.9.b.5.0. to Road R.10.c.

The use of the GHELUWE-MENIN Road WEVELGHEM Road is forbidden.

Copy No. 13
22nd Octr. 1918.

G.638.

102Nd Infantry Brigade.
WARNING ORDER NO. 264.

The 102nd Infantry Brigade Group will move to-morrow morning, the 23rd instant, - leading Unit leaving ST. ANNE about 9 a.m. - to an area EAST of BELLEGHEM, preparatory to taking over the line to-morrow night, 23rd/24th instant.
Detailed orders will be issued later.

W Carr Captain,
Brigade Major,
102nd Infantry Brigade.

Copies to :
1 - 8   8 Units.
  9   B.I.O.
 10   B.S.O.
 11   B.T.O.
 12   Staff Captain.
 ~~13~~14   File.
 1~~4~~5   No. 3 Coy. Train.
 13   34th Division "G".

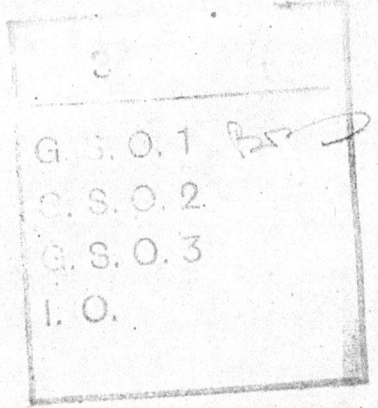

APP VIII

SECRET.
Copy No. 3.

22nd October 1918.

102ND INFANTRY BRIGADE ORDER NO. 234.

Reference Map.
Sheet 29. 1/40,000/

1. With a view to relieving the RIGHT Brigade (124th Infantry Brigade) 41st Division to-morrow night 23rd/24th October, on Front N.18.a. to O.22.c., the 102nd Infantry Brigade Group will move to-morrow morning to the area N.35., O.31., and U.1. in accordance with Table "A" attached. Brigade Group will be in its new area by 11-45.

2. The following distances will be observed on the line of march

   100 yards between Companies.
   25 yards between every six vehicles.

3. Billetting parties and guides will meet Units at Road Junction, N.35.d.0.6. on arrival.

4. Transport of the Brigade Group will be brigaded and move under the orders of the Brigade Transport Officer. Transport will rejoin Units on its arrival in the new area.

5. O.C. "B" Company, Machine Gun Battalion and O.C. 102nd L.T.M.B, will arrange for one section of machine guns and two Stokes mortars respectively to be attached to each Battalion immediately on its arrival in the new area. One Section of Machine Guns and 2 Stokes Mortars will be in Brigade Reserve.

6. Brigade Headquarters will close at ST ANNE at 0930, 23rd inst. and re-open at N.35.d. at a definite place and time to be notified later.

7. ACKNOWLEDGE.

Captain,
Brigade Major,
102nd Infantry Brigade.

Secret.
Copy No. 9.
22nd Octr. 1918.

102nd Infantry Brigade.
WARNING ORDER NO. 214.

The 102nd Infantry Brigade Group will move to-morrow morning, the 23rd instant, - leading unit leaving ST. ANNE about 9 a.m. - to an area EAST of MILLEKRUIS, preparatory to taking over the line to-morrow night, 23rd/24th instant.

Detailed orders will be issued later.

M Carr Captain,
Brigade Major,
102nd Infantry Brigade.

Copies to :
1 - 8   8 Units.
 9   B.I.O.
10   B.S.O.
11   B.T.O.
12   Staff Captain.
13&14   File.
15   No. 5 Coy. Train.
13   34th Division "G".

SECRET.
Copy No......
22nd October 1918.

102ND INFANTRY BRIGADE ORDER NO. 246.

Reference Map.
Sheet 57. 1/40,000.

1. With a view to relieving the RIGHT Brigade (124th Infantry Brigade) 41st Division to-morrow night, 23rd/24th October, on Front O.18.a., to O.22.c., the 102nd Infantry Brigade Group will move to-morrow morning to the area N.30., O.31 and O.1. in accordance with Table "A" attached. Brigade Group will be in its new area by 11-45.

2. The following distances will be observed on the line of march :-

    100 yards between Companies.
    25 yards between every six vehicles.

3. Billeting Parties and guides will meet Units at Road Junction, N.35.d.0.5. on arrival.

4. Transport of the Brigade Group will be brigaded and move under the orders of the Brigade Transport Officer. Transport will rejoin Units on its arrival in the new area.

5. O.C. "D" Coy., Machine Gun Batt. and O.C. 102nd L.T.M.B. will arrange for one section machine guns and two Stokes mortars respectively to be attached to each battalion immediately on arrival in the new area. One Section of Machine Guns and 2 Stokes Mortars will be in Brigade Reserve.

6. Brigade Headquarters will close at MY ARMY at 9-30 a.m., 23rd instant, and re-open at N.36.d. at a definite place and time to be notified later.

7. ACKNOWLEDGE.

> M Carr
> Captain,
> Brigade Major,
> 102nd Infantry Brigade.

TABLE "A" Starting point ARLANCHE CROSS ROAD N.57.c.9.1.

Ser. No.	Unit.	From	To	Starting point. Time head of unit passes starting Pt.	Route	Remarks.
1.	Dismounted Personnel. 1/7th Bn. Cheshire Regt.	ST ANNE	O.31.b.	0940	Road Junction N.26.a.7.9.- BRIASTRE - N.12.c.9.8½.- N.31.d.c.9.	
2	Dismounted Personnel 1/1st Bn. Hereford Regt.	-do-	O.31.c.d.9.	1020	-do-	-do-
3.	Dismounted Personnel 1/4th Bn. Cheshire Regt.	-do-	N.32.d.	1010	Road Junction N.13.c.1.9. - KNOB N.20.d.- thence as for Serial No. 1.	
4.	"C" Coy. 2/4th Som. L.I.	-do-	N.32.b.	1020	as for Serial No. 1.	
5.	Dismounted Personnel "B" Coy. M.G. Batt.	-do-	N.31.b.	1025	-do-	
6.	103rd L.T.M.B. Brigade H.Q.	-do-	N.32.d.	1030	-do-	
7.	Transport, Bde. Group.	-do-	N.32.c.	Not to pass through ST AMES before 0930.	Cross Roads N.31.c.5.8. ROMAERES thence road to be reconnoitred.	Order of march as for Units. Orders will be issued by the Bde. Transport Officer.
8.	203th Fd. Coy. R.E.	-do-	N.32.c.	To follow transport of Bde. Group.	-do-	
9.	96th A.F.A. Brigade.	ARLANCHE	N.32.c.	Not to enter ROMAERES before 1040.	ARLANCHE - ROMAERES thence road to be reconnoitred.	

SECRET.
Copy No. 4..

22nd October 1918.

102ND INFANTRY BRIGADE ORDER NO. 224.

Reference Map.
Sheet 29. 1/40,000/

1. With a view to relieving the RIGHT Brigade (124th Infantry Brigade) 41st Division to-morrow night 23rd/24th October, on Front N.18.a. to O.22.c., the 102nd Infantry Brigade Group will move to-morrow morning to the area N.38., O.31., and U.1. in accordance with Table "A" attached. Brigade Group will be in its new area by 11-45.

2. The following distances will be observed on the line of march
    100 yards between Companies.
    25 yards between every six vehicles.

3. Billetting parties and guides will meet Units at Road Junction, N.38.d.0.8. on arrival.

4. Transport of the Brigade Group will be brigaded and move under the orders of the Brigade Transport Officer. Transport will rejoin Units on its arrival in the new area.

5. O.C. "B" Company, Machine Gun Battalion and O.C. 102nd L.T.M.B, will arrange for one section of machine guns and two Stokes mortars respectively to be attached to each Battalion immediately on its arrival in the new area. One Section of Machine Guns and 2 Stokes Mortars will be in Brigade Reserve.

6. Brigade Headquarters will close at ST AMME at 0930, 23rd inst. and re-open at N.38.d. at a definite place and time to be notified later.

7. ACKNOWLEDGE.

Captain,
Brigade Major,
102nd Infantry Brigade.

TABLE "A". Starting Point BELLEGHEM CROSS ROADS N.27.c.8.1.

Ser. No.	Unit.	From	To	Time head of unit passes starting pt.	Route	Remarks
1.	Dismounted Personnel. 1/7th Bn.Cheshire Regt.	ST ANNE	O.31.b.	0940	Road Junction N.23.c.7.5. BELLEGHEM - N.29.c.0.5 - N.35.d.0.3.	
2.	Dismounted personnel 1/1st Bn.Hereford Regt.	—do—	O.31.c.& d.	100	—do—	
3.	Dismounted personnel 1/4th Bn. Cheshire Regt.	—do—	N.36.d.	1010	Road Junction N.15.c.1.6.— KNOCK N.20.d. — thence as for Serial No. 1.	
4.	'C' Coy. 2/4th Som. L.I.	—do—	N.36.b.	1020	As for Serial No. 1.	
5.	Dismounted personnel "B" Coy M.G.Batt.	—do—	N.36.b.	1025	—do—	
6.	102nd L.T.M.B. and Brigade Hd.Qrs.	—do—	N.36.d.	1030	—do—	
7.	Transport, Bde.Group.	—do—	N.36.a.	Not to pass through ST ANNE before 0950.	Cross Roads N.51.c.8.6. ROLLEGHEM thence road to be reconnoitred.	Order of march as for Units. Orders will be issued by the Bde. Transport Officer.
8.	208th Field Co. R.E.	—do—	N.36.a.	To follow Transport of Bde. Group.	—do—	
9.	96th A.F.A.Brigade.	AELBEKE	N.36.c.	Not to enter ROLLEGHEM before 1045.	AELBEKE - ROLLEGHEM thence road to be reconnoitred.	

Ref. Map.
Sh. 29. 1/40,000.

APP IX

SECRET.
Copy No. 19.

23rd October 1918.

102ND INFANTRY BRIGADE ORDER NO. 265.

1. The 123rd Infantry Brigade, 41st Division, is attacking at 0.2.15., 24th October, starting from the Line O.22.d. - O.23.c. with its Right on the Canal. As soon as its Right has progressed South of the Tunnel in O.23.d. and O.29.b. the 123rd Infantry Brigade will change its direction to SOUTH EAST and its Right will pass just EAST of MOEN. As the rear echelons of the Right Battalion, 123rd Infantry Brigade, change direction, one Battalion of the 102nd Infantry Brigade will fill the gap between the Right of the 123rd Infantry Brigade and the Canal and also advance South with its Right on the Canal and its Left in touch with the Right of the 123rd Infantry Brigade. The remaining Battalions of the 102nd Infantry Brigade will be handled as the situation demands, the object being to gain the WESTERN Bank of the SCHELDT between V.9.c.8.0. and U.18.d.8.0. touch being maintained with the Left of the 30th Division.

2. In order to co-operate with the 123rd Infantry Brigade the action of the Units of the 102nd Infantry Brigade will be as under:-

    (a) After taking over the Line to-night, the 1/1st Battalion Hereford Regiment will move their Support and Reserve Coys. to the Tunnel in O.22.d. and O.23.b., ready for moving across the Tunnel. As this move takes place the two Companies of the 1/4th Battalion Cheshire Regiment will move to the positions vacated by the two Companies of the 1/1st Battalion Hereford Regiment.

    (b) Should the attack of the 123rd Infantry Brigade progress favourably, as soon as the rear of the Right Leading Battn. of the 123rd Infantry Brigade passes the Tunnel, the two Companies of the 1/1st Battalion Hereford Regiment mentioned in sub-para. (a) will move across the Tunnel and follow the Right Battalion 123rd Infantry Brigade. These Companies will keep their Right along the EASTERN Bank of the Canal and as the 123rd Infantry Brigade changes direction to SOUTH EAST they will keep in touch with it filling the gap between the Right of the 123rd Infantry Brigade and the Canal.

    (c) Immediately the two Companies of the 1/1st Battalion Hereford Regiment move across the Tunnel, the remaining two Companies (that is, Front Line Companies) of this Battalion will form up at the Tunnel ready for crossing, the Officer Commanding moving them over when necessary to keep the gap between the Right of the 123rd Infantry Brigade and the Canal Bank filled.

    (d) As soon as the 2 Companies of the 1/1st Battalion Hereford Regiment vacate the Front Line, the 2 Companies of the 1/4th Battalion Cheshire Regiment mentioned in sub-para. (a) will move forward and take up positions vacated by the Front Line Companies of the 1/1st Battalion Hereford Regiment. O.C. 1/4th Battalion Cheshire Regiment will then move his remaining two Companies forward as Support and Reserve to his own Battn.

    (e) The 1/4th Battalion Cheshire Regiment and 1/7th Battalion Cheshire Regiment will not move until the situation develops so as to enable them to swing their Battalions round pivoting on the Right of the 1/7th Battalion Cheshire Regiment. This movement will be carried out by Battalion Commanders concerned as soon as the situation permits.

3. The advance will be continued until the Front Line rests on the NORTH WEST Bank of the SCHELDT between V.9.c.8.0. and U.18.d.8.0.

SHEET 2.

4. The 1/7th Battalion Cheshire Regiment will not extend their Left EAST of the Canal. If the attack is successful the 1/4th Battalion Cheshire Regiment will cross the Canal at the Tunnel or any other crossing found SOUTH of the Tunnel, and if the front of the 1/1st Battalion Hereford Regiment becomes too extended the Officer Commanding the 1/1st Battalion Hereford Regiment will notify the Officer Commanding the 1/4th Battalion Cheshire Regiment who will move forward two Companies to the Right of the 1/1st Battalion Hereford Regiment to fill the gap.

5. Two guns of the 96th A.F.A. Brigade will be earmarked to push forward to a position on the WESTERN Bank of the Canal so as to support the 1/1st Battalion Hereford Regiment and to cover them up to the Final Objective. These guns will be under the orders of the Officer Commanding the 1/1st Battalion Hereford Regiment. The Officer Commanding the 96th A.F.A. Brigade will arrange for the Officer Commanding these guns to be at the Battalion Headquarters of the 1/1st Battalion Hereford Regiment.

6. The Officer Commanding the 1/7th Battalion Cheshire Regiment will arrange to put down a smoke barrage with Stokes Mortars on MOEW and the WOOD in U.18.c. and d. if the situation permits and smoke bombs are available. For this purpose the two Stokes Mortars which are to be attached to the 1/4th Battalion Cheshire Regiment will on completion of their work on the smoke bombs at 0100 report to and come under the orders of the 1/7th Battalion Cheshire Regiment. On completion of the operations they will rejoin the 1/4th Battalion Cheshire Regiment. The two Stokes Mortars attached to the 1/1st Battalion Hereford Regiment will be under the orders of the Officer Commanding this Battalion.

7. The 1/4th Battalion Cheshire Regiment will be prepared to find carrying parties for machine gun ammunition for the 1/1st Battalion Hereford Regiment should they be required.

8. 102nd Infantry Brigade Headquarters at U.1.b.8.5. until further notice.

9. ACKNOWLEDGE.

Captain,
Brigade Major,
102nd Infantry Brigade.

SECRET.
COPY No....21...

102nd. INFANTRY BRIGADE ORDER NO. 256.   23rd October. 1918.

Ref. Map.
SH.29. 1/40.000.

1. The 123rd Infantry Brigade, 41st Division, is attacking at 02.15 on 02.15., 24th October, starting from the Line O.22.d. - O.23.c. with its Right on the Canal. As soon as its Right has progressed South of the Tunnel in O.22.d. and O.28.b. the 123rd Infantry Brigade will change its direction to SOUTH EAST and its Right will pass just EAST of MOEN. As the rear echelons of the Right Battalion, 123rd Infantry Brigade, change direction, one Battalion of the 102nd Infantry Brigade will fill the gap between the Right of the 123rd Infantry Brigade and the Canal and advance SOUTH with its Right on the Canal and its Left in touch with the Right of the 123rd Infantry Brigade. The remaining Battalions of the 102nd Infantry Brigade will be handled as the situation demands, the object being to gain the Western Bank of the SCHELDT between B.9.C.2.0. and U.12.D.8.0. touch being maintained with the left of the 30th Division.

2. In order to co-operate with the 123rd Infantry Brigade the action of the Units of the 102nd Infantry Brigade will be as under

   (a) After taking over the Line to-night, the 1/1st Bn. Hereford Regiment will move their Support and Reserve Companies to the Tunnel in O.22.d. and O.28.b. ready for moving across the Tunnel. As the move takes place two Companies of the 1/4th Bn. Chesire Regt. will move to the positions vacated by the two Companies of the 1/1st Bn. Hereford Regt.

   (b) Should the attack of the 123rd Brigade progress favourably, as soon as the rear of the right leading Battalion of the 123rd Infantry Brigade passes the Tunnel, the two Companies of the 1/1st Bn. Hereford Regt mentioned in sub-para (a) will move across the Tunnel, and follow the right Battalion of the 123rd Infantry Brigade. These Companies will keep their Right along the EASTERN Bank of the Canal, and as the 123rd Infantry Brigade changes direction from to South East they will keep in touch with it, filling the gap between the right of the 123rd Infantry Brigade and the Canal.

   (c) Immediately the two Companies of the 1/1st Bn. Hereford Regiment move across the Tunnel, the remaining two Coys (i.e. Frontt Line Companies) of this Battalion will form up at the Tunnel ready for crossing, the Officer Commanding moving them over when necessary to keep the gap between the right of the 123rd Infantry Brigade and the Canal Bank filled.

   (d) As soon as the two Companies of the 1/1st Bn. Hereford Regiment vacate the front Line, the 2 Companies of the 1/4th Btn Cheshire Regt. mentioned in Sub-para (a) will move forward and take up positions vacated by the front Line Companies of the 1/1st Btn Hereford Regiment. O/C 1/4th Btn Cheshire Regiment will then move his remaining 2 Coys. forward as support and reserve to his own Battalion.

   (e) The 1/4th Btn Cheshire Regiment and 1/7th Btn Cheshire Regiment will not move until the situation develops so as to enable them to swing their Battalions round pivoting on the Right of the 1/7th Btn Cheshire Regiment. This movement will be carried out by Battalion Commanders concerned as soon as the situation permits.

3. The advance will be continued until the Front Line rests on the NORTH WEST Bank of the SCHELDT between V.9.c.2.0. and U.18.d.8.0.

SHEET 2.

4. The 1/7th Btn Cheshire Regiment will not extend their ~~line~~ Left EAST of the Canal. If the attack is successful the 1/4th Bn. Cheshire Regiment will cross the Canal at the Tunnel or any other crossings SOUTH of the tunnel, and if the Front of the 1/1st Battalion Hereford Regiment becomes too extended the Officer Commanding the 1/1st Battalion Hereford Regiment will notify the Officer Commanding the 1/4th Battalion Cheshire Regiment who will move two Companies to the Right of the 1/1st Battalion Hereford Regiment to fill the gap.

5. Two guns of the 96th A.F.A.Brigade will be earmarked to push forward to a position on the WESTERN Bank of the Canal so as to support the 1/1st Battalion Hereford Regiment and to cover them up to the Final Objective. These guns will be under the orders of the Officer Commanding 1/1st Battalion Hereford Regt. The Officer Commanding the 96th A.F.A.Brigade will arrange for the Officer Commanding these guns to be at the Battalion Headquarters of the 1/1st Battalion Hereford Regiment.

6. The Officer Commanding the 1/7th Battalion Cheshire Regiment will arrange to put down a smoke barrage with Stokes Mortars on MOEN and the WOOD in U.18.c. and d., if the situation permits and the smoke bombs are available. For this purpose the 2 Stokes Mortars which are to be attached to the 1/4th Battalion Cheshire Regiment will, on completion of their work on the smoke bombs at 0100 report to and come under the orders of the 1/7th Battalion Cheshire Regiment. On completion of the operations they will rejoin the 1/4th Battalion Cheshire Regiment. The 2 Stokes Mortars attached to the 1/1st Battn. Hereford Regiment will be under the orders of the Officer Commanding this Battalion.

7. The 1/4th Battalion Cheshire Regiment will be prepared to find carrying parties for machine gun ammunition for the 1/1st Battalion Hereford Regiment should they be required.

8. 102nd Infantry Brigade Headquarters will remain at U.1.b.5.3. until further orders.

9. ACKNOWLEDGE.

MCarr
Captain,
Brigade Major,
102nd Infantry Brigade.

SECRET

25th Division G.S.215.

IInd Corps.

Herewith two copies of a report on operations on 10th and 11th August 1917, compiled by G.O.C. 74th Infantry Brigade, for your information. No mention is made in this of the detailed method of advance as it is fully understood within the Division that each wave leapfrogs the one in front of it.

21st Augt 1917.

Major-General,
Commanding 25th Division.

G.S.O.1
G.S.O.2
G.S.O.3
I.O.

F.S.649

copy No. 3

SECRET.

24th October 1918.

102ND INFANTRY BRIGADE ORDER NO. 236.

Reference Map.
Sheet 29, 1/40,000

1. (a) In accordance with 34th Divisional Order No. 269 –
The IInd and XIXth Corps and 34th Division will attack the enemy to-morrow with the object of gaining the Line of the ESCAUT.

    (b) The object of the 34th Division is the River between BOSSUYT (U.24.b) to AUTRYVE (V.9.c.) both inclusive.

    (c) The 41st Division will attack on the Left of the 34th Division. On the Right the 30th Division will maintain their present positions on the ESCAUT, left AT BOSSUYT, exclusive.

2. (a) The attack of the 34th Division will be carried out by the 102nd Infantry Brigade, 96th A.F.A. Brigade, 152nd and 160th F.A. Brigades, and the 34th Battalion Machine Gun Corps (less one Company).

    (b) The remainder of the 103rd Brigade Group will be in Support about BELLEGHEM BOSCH (T.5.a.); remainder of 101st Brigade Group in Reserve about ROLLEGHEMKNOK.

3. (a) The attack will be carried out in accordance with the attached instructions, the main attack will be made from the NORTH in conjunction with the 41st Division, a subsidiary attack being made from S.W. to N.E., South of MOEN, with the object of securing the Crossing over the BOSSUYT CANAL and thence hampering the retreat of the enemy EAST of Canal.

    (b) Main attack will be made under a creeping barrage at the rate of 100 yards in two minutes.
    The subsidiary attack will be made under a smoke screen and will be covered by a standing barrage on Line of MOEN – BOSSUYT Road.
    Machine Guns will co-operate in both attacks.
    The three artillery Brigades and the 34th Battalion Machine Gun Corps will be under Divisional Control.

4. The Advanced Dressing Station is established in BELLEGHEM (N.27.c.8.5).
Main Dressing Station at M.29.d.3.4. in ABEELE.
Car collecting post at T.5.b.2.6.

5. Prisoners of War Cage will be in BELLEGHEM. Prisoners of War should be conducted to Church in BELLEGHEM where Traffic Control will direct them to the Cage.

6. Watches will be synchronised by a Divisional Staff Officer at 102nd Infantry Brigade Headquarters (U.1.b.6.5) at 1800 to-day. Representatives of Infantry and Artillery Brigades and Machine Gun Battalion will attend.

7. A contact patrol aeroplane will fly over the Line at 1000, 1130, and 1300 hours, and flares and discs flashed in reply to calls from the Plane.

8. Advanced Divisional Headquarters will remain in BELLEGHEM.

9. 102nd Infantry Brigade Headquarters will remain at U.1.b.6.5.
All signal arrangements and Battalion and Report Centre Locations will be notified by Brigade Signal Officer in orders issued by him and attached.

10. Boundaries, Starting Line, Pause Line, &c., are shown on Map

Sheet 2.

"A" attached. (Issued to Units of 102nd Infantry Brigade only).

Completion of assembly of 1/4th Battalion Cheshire Regiment and the 1/1st Battalion Hereford Regiment in accordance with instructions issued will be report to Brigade Headquarters by wire by Code Word "IMP". Assembly must be completed so that report of completion reaches Brigade Headquarters by 0600, 25th October.

The 1/7th Battalion Cheshire Regiment will report their dispositions by 0500, 25th October. No change will be made in the dispositions given in this report so as to enable arrangements to be made for the barrage.

11. "M" hour will be 0204 hours, 25th October.

12. ACKNOWLEDGE.

M Carr
Captain,
Brigade Major,
102nd Infantry Brigade.

Distribution :-
1. G.O.C.
2. B.M.
3. S.C.
4. Signalling Officer.
5. Intelligence Officer.
6. 1/4th Bn. Cheshire Regt.
7. 1/7th Bn. Cheshire Regt.
8. 1/1st Bn. Hereford Regt.
9. 102nd L.T.M.B.
10. 34th M.G.Bn.
11. 208th Fd.Coy. R.E.
12. 102nd Field Amb.
13. 34th Division "G".
14. 123rd Brigade.
15. 91st Brigade.
16. 103rd Brigade.
17. 101st Brigade.
18. O.R.A.

19 and 20 War Diary and File.

APPX

SECRET.

24th October 1918.

102nd INFANTRY BRIGADE ORDER NO. 266.

Ref Map:

Sheet No. 1/10,000.

1. (a) In accordance with 34th Divisional Order No. 269 - the IInd and XXIInd Corps and 34th Division will attack the enemy to-morrow with the object of gaining the line of the SCHELDT.

   (b) The objective of the 34th Division is the River between ESCAUT (T.86.b.) to RUPERUS (V.9.c) both inclusive.

   (c) 31st Division will attack on the Left of the 34th Division. On the Right of the 34th Division will maintain their present positions on the ESCAUT, Left at RUMEGNY, exclusive.

2. (a) The attack of the 34th Division will be carried out by the 102nd Infantry Brigade, 85th A.F.A. Brigade, 152nd and 160th R.A.Brigades, and the 34th Battalion Machine Gun Corps (less one Company).

   (b) The remainder of the 103rd Brigade Group will be in Support about RUMEGNY SOUTH (V.3.a); remainder of 101st Infantry Brigade Group in Reserve about BELLIGNIES.

3. (a) The attack will be carried out in accordance with the attached instructions. The main attack will be made from the NORTH in conjunction with the 31st Division, a subsidiary attack being made from G.R. to N.E., South of ROMM, with the object of securing the crossing over the RUMEGNY Canal and thence hampering the retreat of the enemy EAST of canal.

   (b) The main attack will be made under a creeping barrage at the rate of 100 yards in two minutes.
   The subsidiary attack will be made under a smoke screen and will be covered by a standing barrage on line of ROMM - RUMEGNY Road.
   Machine Guns will co-operate in both attacks.
   The three Artillery Brigades and the 34th Battalion Machine Gun Corps will be under Divisional control.

4. The advance dressing station is established in BELLIGNIES (N.27.c.8.5.).
   Main dressing station at N.10.d.6.5. in AUDRET.
   Car Collecting Post at N.1.b.5.5.

5. Prisoners of war Guns will be in BELLIGNIES. Prisoners of war should be directed to the Church in BELLIGNIES where Traffic Control will direct them to the Cage.

6. Watches will be synchronised by a Divisional Staff Officer at 102nd Infantry Brigade Headquarters (N.1.b.4.5.) at 1000 to-day. Representatives of Infantry and Artillery Brigades and Machine Gun Battalion will attend.

7. A contact patrol aeroplane will fly over the line at 1000, 1130, and 1300 hours and fires and discs flashed in reply to calls from the Planes.

8. Advanced Divisional Headquarters will remain in BELLIGNIES.

9. 102nd Infantry Brigade Headquarters will remain at N.1.b.4.5.
   All signal arrangements and Battalion and Report Centre locations will be notified by Brigade Signal Officer in orders issued by him and attached.

10. Boundaries, Starting Line, Forming Line, &c., are shown on

Sheet 2.

"A" attached. (Issued to Units of 102nd Infantry Brigade only).

Completion of assembly of 1/4th Battalion Cheshire Regiment and the 1/1st Battalion Hereford Regiment in accordance with instructions issued will be report to Brigade Headquarters by wire by Code Word "XX". Assembly must be completed so that report of completion reaches Brigade Headquarters by 0200, 23th October.

The 1/7th Battalion Cheshire Regiment will report their dispositions by 0100, 23th October. No change will be made in the dispositions given in this report so as to enable arrangements to be made for the barrage.

11. "Z" hour will be 0904 hours, 23th October.

12. ACKNOWLEDGE.

M Carr
Captain,
Brigade Major,
102nd Infantry Brigade.

Distribution :-
1. G.O.C.
2. S.C.
3. S.C.
4. Signalling Officer.
5. Intelligence Officer.
6. 1/4th Bn. Cheshire Regt.
7. 1/7th Bn. Cheshire Regt.
8. 1/1st Bn. Hereford Regt.
9. 102nd L.T.M.B.
10. 84th M.G.Bn.
11. 208th Fd.Coy. R.E.
12. 102nd Field Amb.
13. 64th Division "G"
14. 192rd Brigade.
15. 31st Brigade.
16. 103rd Brigade.
17. 101st Brigade.
18. C.R.A.

19 and 20 War Diary and File.

SECRET.
24th October 1918.

102ND INFANTRY BRIGADE INSTRUCTIONS NO. 1.

1. The Left Divisional Boundary will be the KNOCKE - KEIBERG - HOSKE Road (exclusive) - V.1.central - V.9.a.0.0.

2. The 102nd Infantry Brigade will relieve troops of the 123rd Infantry Brigade (41st Division) on that portion of the Front between O.22.central and KNOCKE - KEIBERG - HOSKE (exclusive, as soon as possible after dusk this evening. The 1/4th Battalion Cheshire Regiment will carry out this relief disposing his troops in depth so as to have them in the order in which they will advance to-morrow.

3. The Infantry Starting Line of the 102nd Infantry Brigade and the 41st Division is Line O.22.central - O.23.a.7.6. - O.23.a.85.50 - O.23.a.95.95. - O.17.d.6.6. - O.18.a.35.80.

4. The attack will be made under a creeping barrage which will come down 200 yards beyond the above starting line at H - 4 minutes.
    The barrage will start creeping forward at H hour until it reaches the Pause Line shown on attached Map - - - - - at H plus 81 minutes.

5. At H plus 85 minutes the barrage between O.56.c.0.0. and P.31.a.0.0. will cease fire and that on the remainder of the line will continue for ten minutes after H plus 81 and then cease fire.

6. The Village of MOEN will be smoked by field howitzers from H - 4 minutes to H plus 96 minutes during which time the leading troops of the 102nd Infantry Brigade will pass between the village (MOEN) and the Left Divisional Boundary (1/4th Battalion Cheshire Regiment) and join hands with the 1/7th Battalion Cheshire Regiment crossing Canal South of MOEN.
    At H plus 96 minutes the rear echelons of the attacking battalions (two Companies of the 1/1st Battalion Hereford Regiment) will enter MOEN and mop it up.

7. The creeping barrage for the attack is being put down by the 41st Divisional Artillery. The C.R.A., 34th Division, will arrange for two batteries to thicken and extend the barrage in a S.W. direction so as to include the western bank of the Canal as far as O.35.d.6.0.

8. One and a half companies, 34th Bn. Machine Gun Corps, will cover the main attack with a long range barrage according to instructions issued by Officer Commanding, 34th Battalion Machine Gun Corps - issued later.

'B' SUBSIDIARY ATTACK.

1. One Battalion of the 102nd Infantry Brigade (1/7th Battalion Cheshire Regiment) will cross the COURTRAI - BOSSUYT Canal at the most suitable point among the Locks 3, 4, 5, under cover of smoke and field artillery barrage, to be put down by 34th Divisional artillery on the MOEN - BOSSUYT Road at H - 4 minutes, and continue until H plus 81 minutes. This barrage will be thickened so as to form a smoke screen round Locks 3, 4, 5, so as to cover bridging operations.

2. As soon as barrage lifts troops who have crossed canal (1/7th Battalion Cheshire Regiment) will attempt to join hands with those who have passed round Eastern Face of MOEN. (1/4th Battalion Cheshire Regiment.

3. One Machine Gun Company will cover the subsidiary attack
by putting.....

Sheet 2.

by putting down a long range barrage on the line of railway in V.1.c. Farm at D.1.a.8.2. and road through V.7.central from positions about BAVENCHEMKNOK. This barrage will cease at H plus 81.

Half Company, Machine Gun Battalion will, be attached to 1/7th Battalion Cheshire Regiment.

"C" CONTINUATION MAIN ATTACK.

1. The Infantry of the 41st Division are pausing on the above mentioned Pause Line (vide para. "A" 4) from H plus 81 to H plus 81 plus 120 = H plus 201 minutes.

2. At H plus 199 (that is 2 minutes before the end of the pause) a barrage will come down on the Pause Line (marked DOTTED BLUE) from P.31.c.0.0. Northwards only and start to creep forward at H plus 201 minutes at the rate of 100 yards every 2 minutes on the 41st Divisional Front only, until it reaches the line of the ESCAUT.

3. The troops of the 102nd Infantry Brigade (1/4th and 1/7th Battalions Cheshire Regiment having joined hand in V.1.2. will pause on the general line - EASTERN face of MOEN - V.1.central and MOEN - BOSSUYT Road, facing EAST.

4. (a) During this pause the following villages will be kept under fire, which will lift at times stated in the following sub-para. b, at which time the 41st Divisional Barrage lifts is expected to arrive level with them.

(b) MARAILLESTRAAT and HEESTERSTRAAT , North and East of V.7.central at H plus 231 minutes, and AUTRYVE at H plus 251 minutes.

(c) The Village of BOSSUYT East of Canal will not be fired on unless the Officer Commanding 1/7th Battalion Cheshire Regt requests it to be.

5. Heavy artillery will protect our Right.

"D" BATTALION TASKS.

1. The 1/4th Battalion Cheshire Regiment will form up for jumping off on line as detailed shown on Map marked in BLUE. It will be in position, dug in if necessary, by 0500. Officer Commanding Battalion will report to this effect to G.O.C. 102nd Infantry Brigade at that hour by Phone. It then moves forward close under barrage up to the Pause Line shown on map attached marked DOTTED LINE BLUE. At this line the barrage along 1/4th Battalion Cheshire Regiment ceases, but the smoke barrage on MOEN continues. As soon as the barrage lifts from the 1/4th Battalion Cheshire Regiment Front, this Battalion will pass round between EASTERN edge of MOEN and Brigade Left Boundary, circling MOEN so as to join hands with the 1/7th Battalion Cheshire Regiment who should be on EASTERN Bank of Canal about U.12.b.5.5.
If the 1/7th Battalion Cheshire Regiment are not there, they (1/4th Battalion Cheshire Regiment,) will extend to the canal bank. After having joined hands these two Battalions will remain in position detailed approximately in para. 3 of "C" Operation Instructions.

As soon as the 41st Division moves forward under their own barrage the Left of the 1/4th Battalion Cheshire Regiment will move keeping touch with it and the remainder of the Battalion moving forward in a S.E. direction bringing round the 1/7th Battalion Cheshire Regiment with it until they arrive at their Final Objective marked on Map - BROWN. On arrival at the Final Objective, Battalion Commander will re-organise Battalions disposing in depth and digging in.

O.C. 1/4th Battalion Cheshire Regiment must realise that

his actual.....

Sheet 3.

his actual jumping off line is only 250 yards and his actual front after advancing a short distance stretches to 1000 yards, and he must make his plans accordingly so as to be able to extend his front to keep his right on canal and his left in touch with 41st Division, which practically means that he must start crowded.

2. 1/1st Battalion Hersford Regiment. This Battalion will be formed up facing Tunnel in depth, as close to Tunnel as possible (so as to pass through wire where any gap occurs) at 0500, and will report to B.G.C., that this is so at that hour and be prepared to push across tunnel and follow immediately behind the 1/4th Battalion Cheshire Regiment as soon as their rear Company has passed Tunnel. Two Companies will be told off tp support the 1/4th Battalion Cheshire Reg. in close touch, and two companies will be told off to mop up the area over which they travel in rear of the two companies detailed to support the 1/4th Battalion Cheshire Regiment, One of these rear Companies will be specially detailed to mop up MOEN and must push on immediately in rear of the 1/4th Battalion Cheshire Regiment and its two supporting Companies. The other Company will mop up all areas up to MOEN. Special instructions will be issued to each Company, and very strict instructions to all mopping companies that, as soon as their job is complete they will move forward and rejoin their Unit, on the Final Objective forming in rear of the 1/4th and 1/7th Battalion Cheshire Regiment as support.

3. 1/7th Battalion Cheshire Regiment. This Battalion have been particularly detailed in Operation Instructions "C", but Officer Commanding Battalion must bear in mind that if the minor operations of to-night are not successful, that the orders contained in "C" must be followed. Officer Commanding 1/7th Battalion Cheshire Regiment must report his position by 0500, 25/10/18, to B.G.C. and those positions cannot then be altered. This will enable the B.G.C. to notify Division what the situation is and what is required.

4. Two Sections of the Machine Gun Battalion will be at the disposal of the 1/7th Battalion Cheshire Regiment. Officer Commanding these two sections will report to Officer Commanding 1/7th Battalion Cheshire Regiment for dispositions, &c.

5. Four guns of the L.T.M.B. will be placed at the disposal of Officer Commanding 1/7th Battalion Cheshire Regiment. Officer Commanding L.T.M.B. will report to Officer Commanding 1/7th Battalion Cheshire Regiment for instruction.

6. Officer Commanding all Battalions and Units must thoroughly instil into all ranks the absolute necessity of carry out all and every instructions and they must impress on all ranks that they are working with a strange Division and we cannot fail if every officer and man does his part. The task set Brigade is easy and simple provided everyone does his job, otherwise it is difficult and complicated.
Determination and intelligence combined with Esprit de Corps are invincible. Do not spare yourselves and certainly not the enemy. Identifications have been obtained and we need not worry about them.

7. Officer Commanding Machine Gun Battalion and Officer Commanding L.T.M.B., must get their supplies up to-night, as no Infantry Carrying Parties will be supplied on the initial move.

8. Officers Commanding must either by personal observation or the keeping of close touch with the situation see that all

Sheet 4.

instructions are carried out and must be in a position to verify all reports received.

Headquarters will move forward as the situation demands due notification of any move being sent to Brigade Headquarters.

If Battalions are connected to Brigade Headquarters by telephone, Officers Commanding will arrange that an officer is available at all times.

9. The sending back of constant information is of the utmost importance and Officers Commanding will ensure that Brigade Headquarters are kept informed of the progress of the battle. Situation reports will be forwarded to Brigade Headquarters hourly after H hour, and more often when the situation demands it.

Brigadier General,
Commdg. 102nd Infantry Brigade.

APP XI

SECRET.
COPY NO. 21

26th October 1918.

102ND INFANTRY BRIGADE ORDER NO. 287.

Reference Map Sheet 29. 1/40,000.

1. The 102nd Infantry Brigade will be relieved by the 21st Infantry Brigade of the 30th Division on the night 26th/27th October.
   All details will be arranged between Commanding Officers concerned.
   The 102nd Infantry Brigade, on relief, will proceed to the area N.26. – O.21.

2. The 21st Infantry Brigade will take over the line as follows:-
   1/8th Battalion Cheshire Regiment will relieve the 1/7th Battalion Cheshire Regiment on the RIGHT.
   2/23rd Battalion London Regiment will relieve the 1/4th Battalion Cheshire Regiment on the LEFT.
   1/1st Battalion Hereford Regiment will not be actually relieved, but will move from their present position at an hour to be notified later.

   The inter-battalion boundary of the 21st Infantry Brigade will be the BOSSUYT – MOEN Road.

3. Guides to the new areas will meet Units as under:-

   Guides for 1/4th Battalion Cheshire Regiment and 1/1st Battalion Hereford Regiment at road over Canal Tunnel O.26.b.4.7.
   Guides for 1/7th Battalion Cheshire Regiment at road junction O.25.c.5.5.

   Route for outgoing troops :-

   1/4th Battalion Cheshire Regiment and 1/1st Battalion Hereford Regt. via MOENE and Canal Tunnel.
   1/7th Battalion Cheshire Regiment via foot bridge U.12.b.5.7., thence by any route to meeting point with guides.

4. The 206th Field Company, R.E., and "C" Coy. 2/4th Somerset L.I. will remain in their present positions.

5. Completion of relief will be reported by wire to Brigade Headquarters by Code Word "BOOK".
   Brigade Headquarters will remain at U.1.b.5.4.

6. ACKNOWLEDGE.

M Carr
Captain,
Brigade Major,
102nd Infantry Brigade.

Distribution :-
Copy No. 1. G.O.C.
2. B.M.
3. S.C.
4. 1/4th Bn. Cheshire Rgt.
5. 1/7th Batt. Cheshire Rgt.
6. 1/1st Bn. Hereford Rgt.
7. 102nd L.T.M.B.
8. "B" Coy. 34th M.G. Bn.
9. Bde. T.O.
10. 21st Infantry Brigade.
11. 123rd Infantry Brigade.
12. 34th Division "G".
13. 102nd Field Ambulance.
14. 103rd Field Ambulance.
15. No. 3 Company Train.
16. Brigade Supply Officer.
17. 206th Field Company R.E.
18. "C" Coy. 2/4th Som. L.I.
19. Brigade Signalling Officer.
20)
21) War Diary and File.
22 101st Inf Bde
23 103rd Inf Bde

SECRET.
COPY NO. 20

26th October 1918.

102ND. INFANTRY BRIGADE ORDER NO. 227.

Reference Map Sheet 29. 1/40,000.

1. The 102nd Infantry Brigade will be relieved by the 21st Infantry Brigade of the 30th Division on the night 26th/27th October.
    All details will be arranged between Commanding Officers concerned.
    The 102nd Infantry Brigade, on relief, will proceed to the area N.33. - 0.31.

2. The 21st Infantry Brigade will take over the line as follows:-
    1/6th Battalion Cheshire Regiment will relieve the 1/7th Battalion Cheshire Regiment on the RIGHT.
    2/23rd Battalion London Regiment will relieve the 1/4th Battalion Cheshire Regiment on the LEFT.
    1/1st Battalion Hereford Regiment will not be actually relieved, but will move from their present position at an hour to be notified later.

    The inter-battalion boundary of the 21st Infantry Brigade will be the BOSSUYT - MOEN Road.

3. Guides to the new areas will meet Units as under:-

    Guides for 1/4th Battalion Cheshire Regiment and 1/1st Battalion Hereford Regiment at road over Canal Tunnel O.29.b.4.7.
    Guides for 1/7th Battalion Cheshire Regiment at road junction O.33.c.3.3.

    Route for outgoing troops :-

    1/4th Battalion Cheshire Regiment and 1/1st Battalion Hereford Regt. via HOSKE and Canal Tunnel.
    1/7th Battalion Cheshire Regiment via foot bridge U.12.b.3.7., thence by any route to meeting point with guides.

4. The 208th Field Company, R.E., and "C" Coy. 2/4th Somerset L.I. will remain in their present positions.

5. Completion of relief will be reported by wire to Brigade Headquarters by Code Word "BOOK".
    Brigade Headquarters will remain at U.1.b.5.4.

6. ACKNOWLEDGE.

M Carr

Captain,
Brigade Major,
102nd Infantry Brigade.

Distribution :-
Copy No. 1. G.O.C.
2. B.M.
3. S.C.
4. 1/4th Bn. Cheshire Rgt.
5. 1/7th Batt. Cheshire Rgt.
6. 1/1st Bn. Hereford Rgt.
7. 102nd L.T.M.B.
8. "B" Coy. 34th M.G. Bn.
9. Bde. T.O.
10. 21st Infantry Brigade.
11. 123rd Infantry Brigade.
12. 34th Division "G".
13. 102nd Field Ambulance.
14. 103rd Field Ambulance.
15. No. 3 Company Train.
16. Brigade Supply Officer.
17. 208th Field Company R.E.
18. "C" Coy. 2/4th Som. L.I.
19. Brigade Signalling Officer.
20)
21) War Diary and File.

APP XII

SECRET.
Copy No. 2

26th October 1918.

102ND INFANTRY BRIGADE ORDER NO. 268.

Reference Map Sheet 29, 1/40,000.

1. The 102nd Infantry Brigade Group, composed as under, will move to the ST. ANNE Area to-morrow, 27th Instant, in accordance with Table attached.

    102nd Infantry Brigade.
    208th Field Company, R.E.
    "B" Coy. M.G. Battn.
    "C" Coy. 2/4th Somerset L.I.

    All transport will march behind Units.

2. The following distances will be observed on the line of march :-

    100 yards between Battalions.
    100 yards between Companies.
    100 yards between Unit and its Transport.
    25 yards between every six vehicles.

    Units will halt at 10 minutes to the hour.

3. DRESS : Full marching order. Coats will be carried in the packs. Waterproof sheets under the flap of the pack. Steel Helmets under the straps of the pack. Box Respirators will be carried at the 'Alert' position.

    Bands will march at the heads of Battalions. Packs of bands will be carried on the Transport.

4. The usual advance parties from each Unit in the Brigade Group will report to the Staff Captain at ST ANNE at 9 a.m. on the 27th instant.

5. 102nd Infantry Brigade Headquarters will close at U.1.b.4.5., at 10 a.m., and re-open at ST ANNE at an hour to be notified later.

6. ACKNOWLEDGE.

                                            Captain,
                                        Brigade Major,
                                    102nd Infantry Brigade.

Distribution :
Copy No. 1. G.O.C.
       2. B.M.
       3. S.C.
       4. 1/4th Bn. Cheshire Regt.
       5. 1/7th Bn. Cheshire Regt.
       6. 1/1st Bn. Hereford Regt.
       7. 102nd L.T.M.B.
       8. "B" Coy. M.G. Battn.
       9. "C" Coy. 2/4th Som. L.I.
      10. 208th Field Company.
      11. 102nd Field Ambulance. Detachment
      12. 103rd Infantry Brigade.
      13. 101st Infantry Brigade.
      14. 34th Division "G"
      15. No. 3 Company Train.
      16. Brigade Supply Officer.
      17. Brigade Signalling Officer.
      18. Brigade Transport Officer.

      19 & 20 War Diary and File.

SECRET   Copy No..

           102nd Infantry Brigade Order No... 269
Ref. Map
Sheet 28 : 1:40,000.

                                              27 : 10 : 1918.

1..   The 102nd Infantry Brigade Group will move to the
        OYGHEM-HULSTE Area tomorrow, 28th instant, in accordance
        with March Table "A" attached.

2..   All transport will march in rear of Units.
        The following distances will be observed on the line of
march. -

                100 yards between Units.
                100 yards between Companies.
                100 yards between Unit and its transport.
                 25 yards between every six vehicles.

        Units will halt at 10 minutes to the clock hour.

3..   Dress - Full marching order - coats in pack - waterproof
        sheet under flap of pack. Steel helmets will be worn and
        box respirators slung.

        Bands will march at the head of battalions.
                                       be
4.   Marching out states will/handed to a Brigade Staff
        Officer at the Starting Point. Marching in states will be
        forwarded to Brigade Headquarters immediately on arrival
        in new area.

5..   The Staff Captain will issue instructions as to advance
        parties and administrative arrangements.

6..   102nd Infantry Brigade Headquarters will close at
        ST. ANNE at 07.15 on 28th instant and reopen at a time and
        place in the new area to be notified later.

        Acknowledge.
                                                     Captain.
                                              BRIGADE MAJOR.
Distribution -   102nd INFANTRY BRIGADE.
        Copy No. 1 G.O.C.
                 2 Brigade Major.
                 3 Staff Captain.
                 4 1/4th Cheshire Regt.
                 5 1/7th Cheshire Regt.
                 6 1/1st Hereford Regt.
                 7 102nd L.T.M.B.
                 8 "B" Coy. M.G. Bn.
                 9 "C" Coy. 2/4th Som. L.I.
                10 208th Field Co. R.E.
                11 Detachment 102nd Field Amb.
                12 101st Inf. Bde.
                13 103rd Inf. Bde.
                14 34th Div. "G".
                15 No. 3 Coy. Train.
                16 Bde. Supply Off.
                17 Bde. Signal. Officer.
                18 Bde. Transport Officer.

              19 & 20 .. War Diary and File.

March Table "A" to accompany 102nd Infantry Brigade Order No. 289

Starting Point – Road Junction M.12.d.5.7.

Ser. No.	UNIT	FROM	TO	Time head of Units column passes Starting Point	ROUTE	REMARKS
1	102nd Bde. H.Q. 102nd L.T.M.B.	ST. ANNE	OYGHEM HULSTE Area	07.40	M.12.d.5.7. – Cross Roads H.31.b.7.3. – Road along S. of COUTRAI STATION – Railway Crossing H.32.b.1.6. – H.32.a.9.8. – H.27.a.3.3. – Lock No. 9 – STACEGHEM – HARLEBEKE – Bridge H.11.b.central – Cross Roads H.5.c.5.4. – BAVICHOVE.	
2	1/4th Cheshire Regt.	–do–	–do–	07.42.		10 minutes halt while passing Starting Point.
3	1/7th Cheshire Regt.	–do–	–do–	08.0?	–do–	
4	1/1st Hereford Regt.	–do–	–do–	08.2?.	–do–	
5	"B" Coy. M.G. Battalion	–do–	–do–	08.30.	–do–	
6	208th Field Co. R.E.	–do–	–do–	08.36	–do–	
7	2/4th Som. L.I.	–do–	–do–	08.45.	–do–	
8	Detachment 102nd Field Amb.	–do–	–do–	08.48.	–do–	
9	No. 3 Coy. Train.	Present location.	–do–	09.00.	–do–	

SECRET   Copy No..

                102nd Infantry Brigade Order No... 269
Ref. Map
Sheet 28 : 1:40,000.
      29
                                              27 : 10 : 1918.

1..   The 102nd Infantry Brigade Group will move to the
OYGHEM-HULSTE Area tomorrow, 28th instant, in accordance
with March Table "A" attached.

2..   All transport will march in rear of Units.
        The following distances will be observed on the line of
march. -

              100 yards between Units.
              100 yards between Companies.
              100 yards between Unit and its transport.
               25 yards between every six vehicles.

        Units will halt at 10 minutes to the clock hour.

3..   Dress - Full marching order - coats in pack - waterproof
sheet under flap of pack. Steel helmets will be worn and
box respirators slung.

        Bands will march at the head of battalions.
                                      be
4.   Marching out states will/ handed to a Brigade Staff
Officer at the Starting Point. Marching in states will be
forwarded to Brigade Headquarters immediately on arrival
in new area.

5..   The Staff Captain will issue instructions as to advance
parties and administrative arrangements.

6..   102nd Infantry Brigade Headquarters will close at
ST. ANNE at 07.15 on 28th instant and reopen at a time and
place in the new area to be notified later.

        Acknowledge.
                                                    Captain.
                                              BRIGADE MAJOR.
                                         102nd INFANTRY BRIGADE.
Distribution -
        Copy No. 1   G.O.C.
              2   Brigade Major.
              3   Staff Captain.
              4   1/4th Cheshire Regt.
              5   1/7th Cheshire Regt.
              6   1/1st Hereford Regt.
              7   102nd L.T.M.B.
              8   "B" Coy. M.G. Bn.
              9   "C" Coy. 2/4th Som. L.I.
             10   208th Field Co. R.E.
             11   Detachment 102nd Field Amb.
             12   101st Inf. Bde.
             13   103rd Inf. Bde.
             14   34th Div. "G".
             15   No. 3 Coy. Train.
             16   Bde. Supply Off.
             17   Bde. Signal. Officer.
             18   Bde. Transport Officer.

             19 & 20 .. War Diary and File.

March Table "A" to accompany 102nd Infantry Brigade Order No. 269

Starting Point - Road Junction N.12.d.5.7.

Ser. No.	UNIT	FROM	TO	Time head of Units column passes Starting Point	ROUTE	REMARKS
1	102nd Bde. H.Q. 102nd L.T.M.B.	ST. ANNE	OYGHEM HULSTE Area.	07.40.	N.12.d.5.7. - Cross Roads H.31.b.7.4. - Road along S. of COUTRAI STATION - Railway Crossing H.32.b.1.6. - H.32.a.9.8. - H.27.a.5.3. - Lock No. 9 - STACEGHEM - HARLEBEKE - Bridge H.11.b. central - Cross Roads H.5.c.5.4. - BAVICHOVE.	
2	1/4th Cheshire Regt......	-do-	-do-	07.42.		10 minutes halt while passing Starting Point
3	1/7th Cheshire Rgt	-do-	-do-	08.05.	- do -	
4	1/1st Hereford Rgt.	-do-	-do-	08.18.	- do -	
5	"B" Coy. M. "G. Battalion	-do-	-do-	08.31.	- do -	
6	208th Field Coy. R.E.	-do-	-do-	08.38.	- do -	
7	"C" Coy. 2/4th Som. L. I.	-do-	-do-	08.45.	- do -	
8	Detachment 102nd Field Amb	-do-	-do-	08.46.	- do -	
9	No. 3 Coy. Train	Present location.	-do-	09.00.	- do -	

29th Oct. 1918.   SECRET   Copy No....

102nd INFANTRY BRIGADE ORDER NO. 270

Ref Map
Sheet 29 : 1:40,000   APP XIV

1.. The 102nd Infantry Brigade Group will move to HARLEBEKE
     to-day, 29th instant, in accordance with March Table "A"
     attached.
                              Bridge
2.. All transport via N# C.10.a. under orders to be issued
     by Brigade Transport Officer.
     The following distances will be observed on the line of
     march –

            200 yards between Units
            200 yards between Companies
            25 yards between every six vehicles.

     Strict attention will be paid to maintaining of distances.
     Units will halt at 10 minutes to the clock hour.

3.. Dress – Full marching order – Coats in pack. Waterproof
     sheet under flap of pack. Steel helmets will be worn and
     box respirators slung.
     Bands will march at the head of battalions.

4.. Marching out states will be handed to a Brigade Staff
     Officer at the Starting Point. Marching in states will be
     forwarded to Brigade Headquarters immediately on arrival in
     HARLEBEKE.

5.. The Staff Captain will issue instructions as to advance
     parties and administrative instructions, arrangements.

6.. 102nd Inf. Brigade Headquarters will close at OYGHEM at
     10.30 on 29th inst. and reopen at HARLEBEKE at a time to be
     notified later.

7.. Acknowledge.
                                             M Carr
                                                        Captain.
                                              BRIGADE MAJOR
                                          102nd INFANTRY BRIGADE.

Distribution –
     Copy No. 1   G.O.C.
              2   Brigade Major
              3   Staff Captain.
              4   1/4th Cheshire Regt.
              5   1/7th Cheshire Regt.
              6   1/1st Hereford Regt.
              7   102nd L.T.M.B.
              8   "B" Co. M.G.Bn.
              9   "C" Co. 2/4th Som. L.I.
             10   Detachment 102nd Field Amb.
             11   101st Inf. Bde.
             12   103rd Inf. Bde.
             13   505th Field Co. R.E.
             14   34th Division "G".
             15   No. 7 Coy. Train.
             16   Bde. Supply Officer.
             17   Bde. Signalling Officer.
             18   Bde. Transport Officer.

             19 & 20 War Diary and File.

March Table "A" - to accompany 102nd Inf. Bde Order No.220

Starting Point - Cross Roads B.23.d.6.4.

Ser. No.	UNIT.	From	To	Time head of Units column pass starting Point.	Route.	Remarks.
1.	102nd Bde. H.Q.) 102nd L.T.M.B.)	OYGHEM.	HARLEBEKE.	11.28	BAVICHOVE-Cross Rds H.5.c.5.4.- Bridge H.11.b.	
2.	1/1st Hereford Regt.	B.23.d.9.3.	-do-	11.30	do	
3.	1/7th Cheshire Regt.	OYGHEM	-do-	11.40	do	
4.	1/4th Cheshire Regt.	-do-	-do-	12.00	do	
5.	208th Field Co. R.E.) "C" Co. Som. L. I.)	B.18.d.8.1.	-do-	12.10	do	
6.	"B" Co. M. G. Bn....	B.19.a.1.4.	-do-	12.15	do	
7.	Detachment 102nd Field Ambulance	C.7.c.7.9.	-do-	12.20	do	
8.	No. 3 Coy. Train	B.23.d.2.5.	-do-	12.22	do	

TABLE "A" to accompany Brigade Order No. 268. Starting Point, MILL N.35.a.7.6.

Ser. No.	Unit.	From	To	Time head of Column passes Starting Pt	Route	Remarks.
1.	102nd Inf. Bde. H.Q. 102nd L.T.M.B.	U.a.b.4.5.	ST ANNE	10,40	Road Junction T.5.b.3.7. LE CHAT CABT., BELLEGHEM, Road Junction N.32.b.7.8., N.20.central, Cross Roads N.20.a.2.9.	
2.	1/1st Batt. Hereford Rgt.	T.6.	—do—	10,42	—do—	
3.	1/7th Batt. Cheshire Rgt.	O.31.	—do—	11,05	—do—	Will halt while passing Starting Point.
4.	1/4th Bn. Cheshire Regt.	U.1.b.	—do—	11,18	—do—	
5.	"B" Coy. M.G.Battn.	U.1.	—do—	11,31	—do—	
6.	208th Field Coy. R.E.	N.36.	—do—	11,36	—do—	
7.	"C" Coy. 2/4th Som. L.I.	N.36.	—do—	11,40	—do—	
8.	Detachment 102nd F.A.	BELLEGHEM	—do—		—do—	Will join rear of Column as it passes BELLEGHEM.

SECRET.
Copy No......

30th October 1918.

102ND INFANTRY BRIGADE ORDER NO. 171.

Reference Maps :-
 Sheet 29, 1/40,000.
 Sheet 29 N.E. & S.E. 1/20,000.

1. (a) The II and XIX Corps and the 7th French Corps d'Armee will resume the advance at H hour on the 31st October.

   (b) The 31st Division, II Corps will be on the right of the 34th Division and the 41st French Division on the left.

2. (a) The objective lines of the 31st and 34th Divisions will be as shown in RED and BROWN on the attached Map "A".

   (b) The boundary lines between the 34th and 31st Divisions and 34th (Br) and 41st (Fr) Divisions are shown in RED and BROWN on the attached map "A".

3. (a) The attack of the 34th Division will be carried out by the 103rd Infantry Brigade Group (less Arty. and M.G. Coy) plus 1 Battalion, 101st Brigade and two Companies of Tanks of the French Army.

   (b) The attack will be supported by :-

      (i) 34th Divisional Artillery plus 31st and 115th R.A.Bdes. and a proportion of Heavy Artillery.

      (ii) 34th Bn. M.G.Corps (less 1 Company) plus Nos. 1 and 4 Batteries 1st Motor Machine Gun Brigade.

   (c) The 101st Infantry Brigade (less 1 Battalion) will be in support in its present billets.
        The 102nd Infantry Brigade will be in Divisional Reserve in its present billets.

                                              Captain,
                                              Brigade Major,
                                              102nd Infantry Brigade.

Distribution:-
Copy No. 1. G.O.C.
      2. B.M.
      3. S.C.
      4. 1/4th Bn. Cheshire Regt.
      5. 1/7th Bn. Cheshire Regt.
      6. 1/1st Bn. Hereford Regt.
      7. 102nd L.T.M.B.
      8. "B" Coy, 34th M.G.Bn.
      9. 208th Field Coy. R.E.
     10. Brigade Signalling Officer.
     11. Brigade Transport Officer.
     12.)
     13.) War Diary and File.

Wt. W6192/P875 1,500,000 4/18 McA & W Ltd (E 2815) Forms W3091/4.   Army Form W.3091

Cover for Documents.

Nature of Enclosures.

Notes, or Letters written.

VOLUME XXXVI

WAR DIARY
AND
APPENDICES

102ND INFANTRY BRIGADE H.Q.

NOVEMBER - 1918.

[signature]

BRIGADIER GENERAL
CDG. 102ND INFANTRY BRIGADE

Vol XXXIV

WAR DIARY
or
INTELLIGENCE SUMMARY.

REF MAP. TOURNAI 1/100,000

Place	Date	Hour	Summary of Events and Information	Remarks and references to Appendices
HARLEBEKE	Nov 1st		102nd Inf. Brigade billets at HARLEBEKE. Training carried out	
"	2nd		Brigade order No 272 issued l/s a move to MORSEELE Area. Enemy bombed HARLEBEKE billage causing light casualties in Brigade	App I
"	3rd		102nd Inf. Brigade moved to MORSEELE starting 0800 arriving 11.30	
		11.30	Brigade H.Q. opened at MORSEELE	
MORSEELE	4th		Training commenced. Attention devoted to Training of Specialists & practising crossing of rivers.	
"	5th to 13th		Training carried out. Brig. Gen. E. Hillard CMG DSO invalided to England on leave. Lt. Col. Courtenay Hood Commdg. 1/5 B.K.O.S.B. assumed temporary command of the Brigade	

Army Form C. 2118.

WAR DIARY
or
INTELLIGENCE SUMMARY.
(Erase heading not required.)

REF MAP TOURNAI 1/100,000

Place	Date	Hour	Summary of Events and Information	Remarks and references to Appendices
MORSEELE	Nov 13"		Brigade Sports meeting held. Brigade Order No 273 issued orders move to BELLEGHEM area	APP II
BELLEGHEM	14		102nd Inf Bde group moved to BELLEGHEM, POLLEGHEM and starting 0900.	
			Brigade Order No 274 issued	APP III
CELLES	15.		March of Brigade Group continued to CELLES, POTTES area. Brigade order No 275 issued	APP IV
RENAIX	16.		March continued to RENAIX	
" "	17		Brigade Group rested. Brigade Order No. 276 issued.	APP V
FLOBECQ	18		March continued to FLOBECQ - WODECQ area	

WAR DIARY
or
INTELLIGENCE SUMMARY.

Army Form C. 2118.

REF MAP TOURNAI SH 1/100,000

Place	Date	Hour	Summary of Events and Information	Remarks and references to Appendices
FLOBECQ	Nov 19 to Nov 24		Training continued. Ceremonial Route Marching. Practical Training	
"	Nov 25 to Nov 28		1/4th Bn Cheshire Regt. moved from LA PIERRE to FLOBECQ. Location of Units Bde Group. 1/4th Bn. Ches. R. 1/7th Bn. do } FLOBECQ 11th Bn. Herefordshire R. 102nd Field Ambulance No 3 Cy Train 208 Field Cy R.E. BRUYERE	

"	Nov 29th to Nov 30th		G.O.C. 34th Division inspected 102nd Infantry Brigade at FLOBECQ
			Training Continued
			Reinforcements received during month 1/4 th Bn Ches. R. OFF- OR
			13 198
			1/7th " " " 7 189
			11th Herefordshire R.g.
			       Ernest Williams BRIG GENERAL
			       COMMANDING 102ND INF. BDE
				OFF- OR
				29 - 382

Op. Order 272 APP I

1:40,000.

2nd Nov. 1918.

1. The 102nd Infantry Brigade Group composed of Units as shown in March Table "A" will move to MORSEELE tomorrow, the 3rd inst. in accordance with March Table "A" attached.

2. The following distances will be observed on the line of march:

        100 yards between Units.
        100 yards between Companies.
        100 yards between Unit and its Transport.
        25 yards between every six vehicles.

Battalion Headquarters will march with the leading Company and rear party with the Rear Company.

All transport will march in rear of Units.

Units will halt at 10 minutes to the clock hour.

3. Dress - Full marching order - Caps will be worn - overcoats in packs - Waterproof sheets under flaps of packs - steel helmets under the straps of the pack - Box Respirators slung.

4. Marching out states will be handed to a Staff Officer at the Starting Point.
Marching in states will be forwarded to Brigade Headquarters on arrival in new area.

5. The Staff Captain will issue instructions as to advance parties and administrative arrangements.

6. 102nd Inf. Bde. Headquarters will close at HARLEBEKE at 07.30 on 3rd inst, and reopen at MORSEELE at an hour to be notified later.

Acknowledge.

                              Captain.
                         BRIGADE MAJOR
                 102nd INFANTRY BRIGADE.

Distribution -

Copy No. 1 G.O.C.
        2 Brigade Major
        3 Staff Captain.
        4 Bde. Transport Officer.
        5 Bde. Signalling Officer.
        6 1/4th Cheshire Regt.
        7 1/7th Cheshire Regt.
        8 1/1st Hereford Regt.
        9 102nd L.T.M.B.
      10 Detachment 102nd Field Ambulance.
      11 No. 3 Coy. Train.
      12 Bde. Supply Officer.
      13 H.Q. 34th Div.
      14 101st Inf. Bde.

March Table "A" - to accompany 102nd Inf. Bde. Order No. 272   31g:18

Starting Point - LAKHOEK Road Junction H.19.d.7.7.

Serial No.	Unit	From	To	Time Head of Units column passes Starting Point.	Route	Remarks
1	102nd Bde. H.Q. 102nd L.T.M.B.	HAARDEKE	NORBURGH	08.08	Bridge H.19.b.4.4. Road Junction H.11.b.1.9.— LAKHOEK — Bridge H.12.c.9.8. — WATERMOLEN — G.24.a.7.8. — G.20.d.8.2. —	
2	1/7th Cheshire Regt	— do —	— do —	08.11		
3	1/4th Cheshire Regt	— do —	— do —	08.24		
4	1/1st Hereford Regt	— do —	— do —	08.27		
5	Detachment 102nd Field Amb.	DEERLYCK	— do —	09.00		
6	No. 3 Coy. Train	will move independently.				

Secret.

War Diary   APP II
                                                 Copy No. 18

102nd INFANTRY BRIGADE ORDER NO. 273.

Ref. Maps.
Sheet 28 & 29. 1/40,000.   November 13th 1918.

1. The 102nd Infantry Brigade Group composed of Units as under, will move by March Route to the BELLEGHEM-ROLLEGHEM Area tomorrow the 14th inst. in accordance with table "A" attached:-

   102nd Brigade Group..

   102nd Infantry Brigade.
   208th Field Coy R.E.
   2/4th Btn Som.L.I.(Pioneers)
   102nd Field Ambulance.
   No. 3 Coy Divl.train.

2. Distances as laid down in Field Service Regulations Part 1, Sec. 25. will be maintained on the line of march:-

   i.e. 10 yards between companies.
         20 yards between Battalions and Units,
   etc.

   Transport will march in rear of Units.

3. Dress will be full marching order.
   Caps will be worn - Steel Helmets will be carried under the cross straps of the pack.   Box Respirators will be slung.
   Leather Jerkins will be carried folded under the flap of the pack and above the ear-flaps.   Leather Jerkins
   Waterproof sheets will be carried over the Leather Jerkins and under the flap of the pack.

4. The Staff Captain will issue instructions as to advance parties and administrative arrangements.

5. Brigade Headquarters will close at MORSEELE at 0900 and re-open at a place to be notified later on arrival in the new Area.

6. ACKNOWLEDGE.

                                        Captain.
                                     BRIGADE MAJOR.
DISTRIBUTION.   102nd Infantry Brigade.

Copy No. 1. Brigade Commander.
        2. Brigade Major.
        3. Staff Captain.
        4. Brigade Transport Officer.
        5. Brigade Signal Officer.
        6. Brigade Supply Officer.   16. 101st Inf Bde.
        7. 1/4th Btn Cheshire Regt.   17. 103rd Inf. Bde.
        8. 1/7th Btn Cheshire Regt.   18. War Diary.
        9. 1/1st Btn Hereford Regt.   19. File.
       10. 102nd. L.T.M.B.
       11. 208th Field Coy R.E.
       12. 102nd Field Ambulance.
       13. 2/4th Som L.I. (Pioneers)
       14. No. 3 Coy Train.
       15. 34th Division.

MARCH TABLE "A" TO ACCOMPANY 102nd INFANTRY BRIGADE ORDER NO.273.

STARTING POINT 102nd INFANTRY BRIGADE HEADQUARTERS MOORSEELE.

Ser.No.	Unit and order of march.	FROM	TO	Time at which Head of unit passes starting point.	Route.	Remarks.
1.	102nd Inf Bde Headquarters 102nd L.T.M.B.	MOORSEELE	BELLEGHEM ROLLEGHEM Area.	0900	WEVELGHEM, LAUWE, AELBEKE, ROLLEGHEM.	
2.	1/4th.Btn. Cheshire Regt.	do	do	0901	do	
3.	1/7th Btn. Cheshire Regt.	do	do	0907	do	
4.	1/1st Btn. Hereford Regt.	do	do	0913	do	
5.	2/4th Btn. Som.L.I.	WEVELGHEM	do	Will join column as it enters WEVELGHEM.	do	
6.	102nd Field Ambulance.	MOORSEELE	do	0925	do	Must leave space in column for 2/4th. Som.L.I.
7.	No.3 Coy. Train.	do	do	0927	do	
8.	208th Field Coy. R.E.	GYGHEM Area.	do	Will move under orders to be issued separately and join Brigade Group in New Area.		

Secret. Copy No..

102nd Infantry Brigade Order No. 274

APP III
14 : 11 : 1918

Ref. Map -
 TOURNAI - 1:100,000

1. The 102nd Infantry Brigade Group will continue its march tomorrow, Nov. 15th, in accordance with March Table "A" attached.

2. Detailed orders will be the same as laid down for today in Brigade Order No. 273.
 Attention is directed to the necessity of complying with orders as to turn-out and dress. Box respirators will be carried slung over the right shoulder and not on top of the pack.

3. Brigade Headquarters will close at BELLEGHEM at 08.30 and re-open on arrival in new area.

Acknowledge.

Distribution -

 As for Brigade Order No. 273.

Captain.
BRIGADE MAJOR.
102nd INFANTRY BRIGADE

March Table "A" to accompany 102nd Bde. Order No. 27.
Starting Point - Cross Roads Just EAST of H in BELLERIEU (Sh. MOURMAL)

Ser. No.	Unit and order of march	From	To	Time at which head of Unit passes Starting Point.	Route.
1	102nd Inf.Bde H.Q. 102nd L.T.M.B.	BELLERIEU	ORIGNY POTTES REJET MOULSEX BASSE PLAINE FERM.	09.00	99PENEM Road through A in SAVES BELGHIN Bridge- POTTES.
2	1/7th Bn. Cheshire Regt.	-do-	-do-	09.01	-do-
3	1/6th Bn. Cheshire Regt.	-do-	-do-	09.07	-do-
4.	1/1st Bn. Hereford Regt.	BELLERIEU	-do-	09.15	-do-
5.	2/4th Regt. Somerset L.I.	-do-	-do-	09.19	-do-
6.	208th Field Coy. R.E.	-do-	-do-	09.21	-do-
7.	No. 3 Coy. Train.	-do-	-do-	09.30	-do-
8.	102nd Field Ambulance.	BELLERIEU.	-do-	09.55	-do-

SECRET.   Copy No. 19

102nd Infantry Brigade Order No ... 275

Ref. Map
TOURNAI - 1:100,000.   15 : 11 : 1918.

1..   The 102nd Infantry Brigade Group will continue its
        march tomorrow, 16th instant, in accordance with Table "A"
        attached.

2..   Brigade Headquarters will close at CELLES at 10.00
        and reopen on arrival in the new area.

        Acknowledge.

                                                        Captain.
                                                    BRIGADE MAJOR.
Distribution -   102nd INFANTRY BRIGADE.

        As per Brigade Order No. 274.

Table "A" - to accompany 102nd Infantry Brigade Order No... 275

Starting Point :: Road Junction at Milestone 13 on TOURNAI-RENAIX Road.

Nr.	UNIT	From	To	Time head of Unit passes Start Point.	Route	Remarks.
1	102nd Inf.Bde. H.Q. 102nd L.T.M.B.	CELLES	RIGAUDIN, PONT D'ELLEZELLES, BEAUFAUX, MARIVE, RENAIX(S. of WATTRIPONT-ELLEZELLES Road) Area.	10.30	CELLES - ANSERDEUL - RENAIX	
2	1/4th Battn. Cheshire Rgt.	-do-	-do-	10.51	-do-	
3	1/7th Battn. Cheshire Rgt.	-do-	-do-	10.57	-do-	
4	2/4th Battn. Som. L.I.	POTTES	-do-	10.43	-do-	Route from POTTES to CELLES - Road Junction 100 yds. North of X in MOLHUX - Road Junction 400 yds South of 1st T in POTTES - Rd. 700yd South of S in POTTES - Mill 330 yds. N.N.W. of C in CELLES.
5	1/1st Battn. Hereford Rgt.	-do-	-do-	11.00	-do-	
6	208th Field Co. R.E.	-do-	-do-	11.06	-do-	
7	102nd Field Ambulance	CELLES	-do-	11.11	-do-	
8	No.3 Coy.Train	-do-	-do-	11.16	-do-	

Secret.   ADP V   Copy No. 18

17th November 1918.

102ND INFANTRY BRIGADE ORDER NO. 276.

Reference Map. Sheet TOURNAI, 1/100,000.

1. In accordance with the terms of the Armistice, the occupied portions of FRANCE, BELGIUM and LUXEMBURG are to be evacuated by the enemy by the 26th November 1918.
   The country to the German Frontier has been divided into 5 Zones, and the enemy has been instructed to be clear of each Zone on the day preceeding the commencement of the march of the Cavalry Corps into that Zone, i.e., 2 days before it is entered by the leading Division of the II Corps.

2. The Second Army, consisting of the Cavalry Corps (less 1 Division) II, III, XXII and Canadian Corps will begin its advance to the German Frontier on the 17th November 1918.
   The Cavalry Corps will cover the advance and be followed by the Canadian Corps on the right and II Corps on the left, one day's march in rear.
   The III and XXII Corps will follow at a later date.

3. On the 17th November the Cavalry Corps will advance through the present Outpost Line.

4. On the 18th November the ~~Cavalry~~ II Corps will ~~advance~~ begin its march and will move in the following order :-

   1st Echelon - (41st Division - Left.
                   (29th Division - Right.

   2nd Echelon - (9th Division - Left.
                   (34th Division - Right.

   3rd Echelon - II Corps H.A. Group.

5. The march of the 102nd Infantry Brigade Group will be continued to-morrow in accordance with the March Table "A" attached.
   Detailed Orders will be the same as laid down in Brigade Order No. 273.

6. 102nd Infantry Brigade Headquarters will close at RENAIX at ~~08000~~ 02.00, and re-open at FLOBECQ on arrival.

7. ACKNOWLEDGE.

                                        Captain,
                                        Brigade Major,
                                        102nd Infantry Brigade.

Distribution as per Brigade Order No. 273 dated 13/11/1918.

MARCH TABLE "A" - to accompany 102nd INF. BDE. ORDER NO. 278

Ser. No.	Unit.	From	To	Starting Point.	Time head of Unit passes Starting Pt.	Route	Remarks
1.	102nd Inf. Bde. H.Q. 102nd L.T.M.B.	RENAIX	MODERN WODECQ Area.	Railway Crossing 500X N. of RENAIX on the RENAIX-ELLEZELLES Road.	09.00	RENAIX-ELLEZELLES-WODECQ. ELOUCQ Road, the ELLEZELLES-WODECQ Road.	Units proceeding to WODECQ Area villages
2.	1/1st Battn. Hereford Regt.	-do-	-do-	-do-	09.04	-do-	-do-
3.	2/4th Battn. Somerset L.I. (Pioneers)	-do-	-do-	-do-	09.07	-do-	-do-
4.	1/7th Battn. Cheshire Regt.	-do-	-do-	-do-	09.13	-do-	-do-
5.	102nd Field Ambulance	-do-	-do-	-do-	09.19	-do-	-do-
6.	1/4th Battn. Cheshire Regt.	MONT D' ELLEZELLES.	WODECQ	Road Junction 500X due S. of 1st E in ELLEZELLES.	10.00	ELLEZELLES-WODECQ Road.	Not to enter ELLEZELLES before 09.30
7.	208th Field Co. R.E.	BEAUBAIX	Area to be notified later.	-do-	10.00	BEAUBAIX-HIGHANDRE-ELLEZELLES Road.	-do-
8.	No. 3 Coy. Train	CINQUANT	-do-	-		-do-	Will follow Field Ambulance as it passes 56 Kilometer Stone on RENAIX-ELLEZELLES Road.

ALL LORRIES OF UNITS MUST BE EAST OF ROADS ROAD LA HAMAIDE – MODECQ BY 09.00

(6392) Wt. W6192/P875 1,500,000 4/18 McA & W Ltd (E 2815) Forms W3091/4.   Army Form W.3091

Cover for Documents.

Nature of Enclosures.

Notes, or Letters written.

SECRET

VOLUME XXXVII

WAR DIARY
&
APPENDICIES

102ND INFANTRY BRIGADE HEADQUARTERS

DECEMBER - 1918

Edward Kellham

Brigadier General
Commanding 102nd Infantry Brigade

(6392) Wt. W6192/P875 1,500,000 4/18 McA & W Ltd (E 2815) Forms W3091/4.   Army Form W.3091.

Cover for Documents.

Nature of Enclosures.

Notes, or Letters written.

WAR DIARY or INTELLIGENCE SUMMARY

Army Form C. 2118.

Place: TOURNAI 1/100,000
Ref^{ce} MAP: TOURNAI 1/100,000

Place	Date	Hour	Summary of Events and Information	Remarks and references to Appendices
	1918			
FLOBECQ	Dec 1st	10.30	Brigade C.of E. Parade Service	
"	Dec 2nd to Dec 10		Training carried out Battalion Drill, Ceremonial Route Marching + Physical Training	
"	Dec 11th		G.O.C. 34th Division presented Medal Ribbons to recipients in the Brigade. 400 O.R. from 3 Battalions of Brigade + how Powers Bath. left for Brown detachment with 103rd F.A. + 208th Field Coy. R.E. Brigade Order No 277 issued with reference to Move to NAMUR - CHARLEROI Area.	App
"	Dec 13th		102nd Inf. Bde. Group moved from FLOBECQ to GHISLENGHIEN - GIBECQ Area.	
SILLY	Dec 13th		Brigade Group remained in GHISLENGHIEN - GIBECQ Area. Brigade Order No 278 + amendments issued.	App
"	Dec 14th		Brigade Group moved from GHISLENGHIEN - GIBECQ Area to SOIGNIES	

Army Form C. 2118.

WAR DIARY
or
INTELLIGENCE SUMMARY.
(Erase heading not required.)

REF MAPS
BRUSSELS. NAMUR 1/100,000

Place	Date	Hour	Summary of Events and Information	Remarks and references to Appendices
SOIGNIES	Dec 15th		Brigade Group remained in SOIGNIES. Brigade Order No 279 issued.	APP
—	Dec 16		Brigade Group moved to HAINE ST PIERRE – HAINE ST PAUL Area. Brigade Order No 280 issued.	APP
HAINE ST PIERRE	Dec 17th		Brigade Group moved to MONCEAU SUR SAMBRE – DAMPREMY Area. Brigade Order No 281 issued.	APP
MONCEAU	Dec 18th		Brigade Group moved to CHATELET. Brigade Order No 282 issued.	APP
CHATELET	Dec 19th		Brigade Group moved to FOSSE–VITRIVAL Area. 24th Bn. Jn L.I. & 208th Field Cy R.E. left Brigade Group & proceeded to R.E. Group at LESVES. 113 Bde AFA & 34th Divisional DAC came into Brigade Area.	

Army Form C. 2118.

WAR DIARY
or
INTELLIGENCE SUMMARY.
(Erase heading not required.)

REF. MAP NAMUR 1/20,000

Place	Date	Hour	Summary of Events and Information	Remarks and references to Appendices
FOSSE	Dec 19th		Dispositions of Units	
			102nd Inf Bde H.Q. FOSSE	
			14th Bn. Ches. Regt BIESMONT & VITRIVAL — 13 Bde AFA BAMBOIS	
			17th " FOSSE — GRAUX	
			1/1st Bn Hospital Pvt. do — D.A.C. ST GERARD	
			102nd Field Ambulance do	
			102nd L.T.M.B. do	
..	Dec 20th to Dec 25th		Training carried out. Ceremonial Drill. Route Marching — Physical & Recreational Training	
..	Dec 25th		Brig Gen Williams CMG DSO proceeded to Paris on leave. Lt Col Courtenay Hood Commdg 4/5th Bn KOSB 103rd Inf Bde assumed temporary command of the 102nd Inf Brigade	

Ernest Williams
Brigadier General
Commanding 102 nd Inf Bde

APP I

SECRET.
Copy No. 18.

102ND INFANTRY BRIGADE ORDER NO. 277.

11th December 1918.

Reference Maps — TOURNAI)
                BRUSSELS) 1/100,000
                NAMUR   )

---

1. The 34th Division will commence its move to the new area S.W. of NAMUR on the 12th instant.

2. The 102nd Infantry Brigade Group will be constituted as follows:-

    102nd Infantry Brigade.
    208th Field Company, R.E.
    2/4th Bn. Somerset L.I.
    102nd Field Ambulance.
    No. 2 Company, Divl. Train.

3. The move of the 102nd Infantry Brigade Group will be carried out in accordance with the following programme :-

    "B" Day, move to GHISLENGHIEN - GIBECQ Area.
    "C" Day, halt in   -do-   -do-
    "D" Day, move to SOIGNIES - NAAST Area.
    "E" Day, halt in   -do-   -do-
    "F" Day, move to LA HESTRE Area.
    "G" Day, to an area to be notified later.
    "H" Day, move to an area to be notified later.
    "I" Day, move to the FOSSE-VITRIVAL - ST. GERARD Area.

    "B" day will be the 12th instant, "C" day the 13th instant, and so on.

4. (a) The 102nd Infantry Brigade Group will commence its march on the 12th instant in accordance with Table "A" attached.
         Distances to be maintained on the line of march will be as laid down in Fourth Army G.S. 128 dated 15/11/1918 issued to Units of 102nd Infantry Brigade under this office No. T.S.42/121 of the 8th instant.

         Units will halt at 10 minutes to the clock hour.

    (b) Dress : Full marching order. Steel Helmets will be carried under the cross straps of the Pack. Box Respirators on top of the pack. When carried on the man leather jerkins will be carried folded under the flap of the pack but above the ear flap. Waterproof sheets will be carried folded separately and carried over the leather jerkin under the flap of the pack. Mess tins will be inside the pack.

    (c) The Staff Captain will issue instructions as to advance parties, transport for baggage, and administrative arrangements Advance parties will meet units on arrival on the 12th inst. at the level crossing just North of GHISLENGHIEN.

    (d) Brigade Headquarters will close at ELOBECQ at 09.00 hours on the 12th instant, and re-open in the new area on arrival.

5. ACKNOWLEDGE.

                                      (signed)
                                      Captain,
                                      Brigade Major,
                                      102nd Infantry Brigade.

Distribution - P.T.O.

DISTRIBUTION.

Copy No. 1.   G.O.C.
2.   B.M.
3.   S.C.
4.   Brigade Transport Officer.
5.   Brigade Signalling Officer.
6.   Brigade Supply Officer.
7.   1/4th Bn. Cheshire Regt.
8.   1/7th Bn. Cheshire Regt.
9.   1/1st Bn. Hereford Regt.
10. 105nd L.T.M.B.
11. 203th Field Company, R.E.
12. 2/4th Bn. Somerset L.I.
13. 102nd Field Ambulance.
14. No. 3 Company Train.
15. 34th Division "Q".
16. 101st Infantry Brigade.
17. 103rd Infantry Brigade.
18.) War Diary and File.
19.)

MARCH TABLE "A" to accompany 102nd Infantry Brigade Order No. 277.

Starting Point - Junction of main road just S.E. of OGY Church.

Ser. No.	Unit.	From	To	Time head of Unit column passed S.P.	Route.	Remarks.
1.	Brigade H.Q. 102nd L.T.M.B.	FLOBECQ,	GHISLENGHIEN Area.	09.49.	OGY - LESSINES - GHISLENGHIEN.	
2.	1/4th Bn. Cheshire Regt.	-do-	-do-	09.52	-do-	
3.	1/7th Bn. Cheshire Regt.	-do-	-do-	10.00	-do-	
4.	1/1st Bn. Hereford Regt.	-do-	-do-	10.07	-do-	
5.	2/4th Bn. Somerset L.I.	WODECQ	-do-	10.14	-do-	
6.	208th Field Coy. R.E.	WODECQ	-do-	10.21	-do-	
7.	102nd Fd. Amb.	FLOBECQ.	-do-	10.28	-do-	
8.	No. 5 Coy. Div. Train.	-do-	-do-	10.31	-do-	

All lorries of the Brigade Group must be clear of ATH - WODECQ and SOIGNIES - GHISLENGHIEN Road by 8-45. Lorries of the 102nd Infantry Brigade will rendezvous, on the 13th instant in the Square, FLOBECQ, at 07.45, ready loaded.

SECRET.

13th December 1918.

AMENDMENT NO. 2 to 102nd INFANTRY BRIGADE ORDER NO. 278.

Column 4 of March Table "A", for "SOIGNIES - NAAST Area" read "the whole of the village of SOIGNIES up to the 19 kilometer stone North and exclusive of the MONS - BRAIN LE COMTE Road."

The Staff Captain will arrange to collect advance parties despatched to-day, the 13th instant, and allot new area.

Captain,
Brigade Major,
102nd Infantry Brigade.

SECRET.
Copy No...19..

13th December 1918.

AMENDMENT NO. 1 to 102ND INFANTRY BRIGADE ORDER NO. 278.

1. Times in column 8 of March Table "A" will be retarded one hour, i.e., Ser. No. 1, 102nd Inf.Bde.HQ. and 102nd L.T.M.B. passes Starting Point at 10.00 hours, and so on.

   Amend times for lorries as follows:-

   All lorries must be clear of MASH by 09.30 and must not not pass the tail of the 101st Infantry Brigade.

   Lorries will rendezvous, ready loaded, at the Starting Point at 08.30.

2. ACKNOWLEDGE BY BEARER.

                                        Captain,
                                        Brigade Major,
                                    102nd Infantry Brigade.

To all recipients of B.O.278.

SECRET.
Copy No....19....

13th December 1918.

102ND INFANTRY BRIGADE ORDER NO. 278.

Reference Maps - TOURNAI)
                    BRUSSELS) 1/100,000.
                    NAMUR   )

1.   The 102nd Infantry Brigade Group will continue its march on the 14th instant in accordance with March Table "A" attached.

2.   Detailed Orders will be as laid down in Brigade Order No. 277 dated the 11th instant.
      Advance parties will meet incoming units at Road Junction at 19 Kilometer stone N.W. of SOIGNIES.

3.   102nd Infantry Brigade Headquarters will close at SILLY at 08.30, and re-open on arrival in the new area.

4.   ACKNOWLEDGE.

                                          Captain,
                                    Brigade Major,
                            102nd Infantry Brigade.

Distribution as per Brigade Order No. 277 dated the 11th instant.

MARCH TABLE "A" to accompany Brigade Order No. 275.

Starting Point - Road Junction ½ mile S.E. of KRAS

Ser. No.	Unit.	From	To	Time head of column passed Starting Point.	Remarks.
1.	Bde. H.Q. Sig. Coy. Bde. M.G. Bn.	BETHEM	BETHEM - NAAST AREA	08.00	
2.	30th Fd. Coy.R.E.	—do—	—do—	08.03	
3.	18th Fd Ambce.	—do—	—do—	08.07	3 ambulances to be detailed to meet in rear of Adv. Gd.Bn.
4.	1/4th Bn. Bedford Regt.	—do—	—do—	08.11	
5.	2/4th Bn. Suffolk Regt.	BETHLEHEM	—do—	08.19	
6.	2/4th Bn. Chadire Regt.	BETHLEHEM	—do—	08.23	
7.	1/7th Bn. Chadire Regt.	BETHLEHEM	—do—	08.33	
8.	No. 3 Coy. Div. Train.	BAK	—do—	08.40	

All lorries must be clear of road junction ½ mile S.W. of SOIGNIES STATION by 08.45.

They will rendezvous headed at the starting point at 07.30.

SECRET. 18.
Copy No. ....
15th December 1918.

102ND INFANTRY BRIGADE ORDER NO. 279.

Reference Maps :- } 1/100,000.
                  } FRASNES

1. The 102nd Infantry Brigade Group will continue its march on the 16th instant in accordance with March Table "A" attached.

2. Detailed orders will be the same as laid down in Brigade Order No. 277 dated the 11th instant.

   Attention is directed to the last paragraph of Fourth Army G.S. 123 with reference to compliments on the line of march.

   Advance parties will meet incoming units at ERBIX.

3. Brigade Headquarters will close at MOIGNIES at 07.30 on the 16th instant and re-open on arrival in the new area.

4. ACKNOWLEDGE.

             M Carr
                    Captain,
                    Brigade Major,
                    102nd Infantry Brigade.

Distribution - As per Brigade Order No. 277.
               Copy to Officer I/c Lorries.

APP III

MARCH TABLE "A" to accompany Brigade Order No. 279.

Starting Point - HAUT POLLIS Cross Roads 200 yards due S. of kilometer stone 20 on the SOIGNIES-ROEULX Road.

Ser. No.	Unit.	From	To	Time head of Units Column passes Stg. Pt.	Route	REMARKS.
1.	102nd Inf.Bde.H.Q. 102nd L.T.M.B.	SOIGNIES.	LA HESTRE Area	08.27 ~~09.00~~	ROEULX-LA-LOUVIERE.	
2.	1/7th Bn. Cheshire Rgt.	-do-	-do-	08.29 ~~09.02~~	-do-	
3.	1/1st Bn. Hereford Regt.	-do-	-do-	08.36 ~~09.09~~	-do-	
4.	1/4th Bn. Cheshire Regt.	-do-	-do-	08.43 ~~09.16~~	-do-	
5.	203th Field Coy. R.E.	-do-	-do-	09.00 ~~09.25~~	-do-	
~~766.~~	102nd Field Ambulance.	-do-	-do-	09.05 ~~09.22~~	-do-	2 ambulances to be detailed to march in rear of Brigade column.
7.	No. 3 Coy. Div. Train	-do-	-do-	09.10 ~~09.35~~	-do-	
8.	2/4th Bn. Somerset L.I.	-do-	-do-	~~09.17~~ 09.13	-do-	

All lorries must be clear of Railway Crossing at HOUPENG-AULNERIES Station by 08.10.

Lorries will be loaded by 07.00.

SECRET. Copy No .....
16th December, 1918.

102ND INFANTRY BRIGADE ORDER NO. 380

APP IV

Reference Maps – NAMUR }
                BRUSSELS } 1/100,000

1. The 102nd Infantry Brigade Group will continue its march on the 17th instant in accordance with March Table "A" attached.

2. Detailed orders will be the same as laid down in Brigade Order No 377 dated 11th instant.
   Advance parties will meet incoming Units at HOUGRAU-SUR-MAINES.

3. Brigade Headquarters will close at HAMME ST PIERRE at 07.30 and reopen on arrival in the new area.

4. ACKNOWLEDGE.

                                        Captain,
                                        Brigade Major,
                                        102nd Infantry Brigade.

Distribution as per Brigade Order No 377.

MARCH TABLE "A" to accompany Brigade Order No 250.

Starting Point - MANIN Cross Roads 400 yards N of R in MANSUY Station on the
LA HERIE - CHIPPEAU LEZEMMAINES ROAD.

Ser. No.	Unit	From	To	Time head of Units Column passes St. Point	Route	Remarks
1.	163rd Brigade H.Q. 163rd I.T.M.B.	LA HERIE A.4.d.	DAMERIES R.10.c.1 to R.10.c. Amb.	08.40 hours	DAMERIES - SAULZOIR - SOLESMES.	
2.	1/4th Cheshire Regt.	-do-	-do-	08.50	-do-	
3.	1/7th Cheshire Regt.	-do-	-do-	08.55	-do-	
4.	1/2nd Hereford Regt.	-do-	-do-	09.10	-do-	
5.	250 Field Coy. R.E.	-do-	-do-	09.25	-do-	
6.	163rd Field Ambulance	-do-	-do-	09.20	-do-	The Ambulance is to detailed to march in rear of 250 RE.
7.	No 3 Coy.Div.Train.	-do-	-do-	09.30	-do-	
8.	B/4th Br. Coumort L.T.	-do-	-do-	09.35	-do-	

SECRET.
Copy No......
17th December. 1918.

102ND INFANTRY BRIGADE ORDER NO. 281.

Reference Map - NAMUR 1/100.000.

1. The 102nd Infantry Brigade Group will continue its march on the 18th instant in accordance with March Table "A" attached.

2. Detailed orders will be the same as laid down in Brigade Order No. 277 dated the 11th instant.
   Advance parties will meet incoming Units at C in Ciding on the COUILLET-CHATELET Road.

3. Brigade Headquarters will close at MONCEAU at 09.00 and re-open on arrival in the new area.

4. ACKNOWLEDGE.

[signature]

Captain,
Brigade Major,
102nd Infantry Brigade.

Distribution - as per Brigade Order No. 277.

MARCH TABLE "A" to accompany Brigade Order No. 231.

Starting Point - Road Junction 400 yards South of Y in DAIPURI.

Ser. No.	Unit	From	To	Time head of Unit's Column passes Stg. Pt.	Route.	Remarks.
1.	102nd Inf. Bde. H. Q. 102nd L.T.M.B.	BONCHAU.	CHANLEDT.	10.10	CHANLEDT-LARCHERES-CHESNAY.	
2.	2/4th Bn. Somerset L.I.	DAIPURI.	-do-	10.13	-do-	
3.	208th Field Company R.E.	BONCHAU.	-do-	10.19	-do-	
4.	1/4th Bn. Cheshire Regt.	LARCHERES AU PONT.	-do-	10.24	-do-	
5.	1/7th Bn. Cheshire Regt.	-do-	-do-	10.31	-do-	
6.	1/1st Bn. Hereford Regt.	BONCHAU.	-do-	10.39	-do-	
7.	102nd Field Ambulance.	-do-	-do-	10.45	-do-	
8.	No. 3 Coy. Dv. Train.	-do-	-do-	11.00	-do-	

Lorries will rendezvous, loaded, at the Starting Point at 07.45.

Copy No. ......

18th December 1918.

102ND INFANTRY BRIGADE ORDER NO. 282.

Reference Map - NAMUR 1/100,000.

1. The 102nd Infantry Brigade Group will continue its march on the 19th instant in accordance with March Table "A" attached.

2. Detailed orders will be the same as laid down in Brigade Order No. 277 dated the 11th instant.

3. Brigade Headquarters will close at GIVERLET at 07.00 hours and re-open on arrival at FOSSE.

4. ACKNOWLEDGE.

Captain,
Brigade Major,
102nd Infantry Brigade.

Distribution - As per Brigade Order No. 277.

MARCH TABLE "B" to Company Orders No. 233.

Starting Point. - Road Junction at #7 Kilometer stone on the PARIS-CHARTRES Road.

Ser No.	Unit	From	To	Time to clear/ Arrive at Starting Point/Point 24-24.	Route	Remarks
	10 Sqn			08.00	P1.24-24-T19.04/ec-Paris	Will use three orders of C.R.P. on arrival at destination.
	11 Sqn L.G. ...			08.15		
	2/Lt. Hr. Sommers.	CLERMONT	REIMS	08.30		
	PLAN OF CONVOY					
	7/Fr. Lt. ...			08.15		
	7/Fr. ...			08.30		
	8/Fr. Chauffeur ...			08.45		
	Ord.			09.00		
	No. 4 Coy. H.T.			09.15		

Lorries will rendezvous loaded, at the Starting point at 07.15 hours.

WAR DIARY
AND APPENDICES

102ND INFANTRY BRIGADE HEADQUARTERS

JANUARY - 1919

Brigadier General
Commanding 102nd Inf. Brigade

Army Form C. 2118.

WAR DIARY
or
INTELLIGENCE SUMMARY.
(Erase heading not required.)

102nd Infantry Brigade H.Q.

Instructions regarding War Diaries and Intelligence Summaries are contained in F.S. Regs., Part II. and the Staff Manual respectively. Title pages will be prepared in manuscript.

Place	Date	Hour	Summary of Events and Information	Remarks and references to Appendices
~~FOSSE~~	1/1/19		The Brigade was billetted in the FOSSE Area and distributed as follows:—	M.
			1/4th Bn. Cheshire Regiment - VITRIVAL and AISEMONT.	
			1/7th Bn. Cheshire Regiment)	
			1/1st Bn. Hereford Regiment) - FOSSE.	
			102nd Infantry Brigade H.Q.)	
	2/1/19		On the 2nd instant the Corps Commander inspected Battalions.	M.
	17/1/19		The Brigade was inspected by the Brigadier General Commanding and "March Past" with Colours at FOSSE.	M.
	18/1/19		The Divisional Commander inspected the Brigade at FOSSE, and presented ribbons to recipients of medals.	M.
	22/1/19		The Brigade relieved the 6th Canadian Infantry Brigade in the BONN area (RHINE) leaving FOSSE on the 21st instant, and proceeded by train to OBERCASSEL (4 miles South of BONN). Battalions relieved as follows:—	M.
			1/7th Bn. Cheshire Regt. relieved 19th Canadian Infantry Battalion.	
			1/4th Bn. Cheshire Regt. relieved 1st Battalion Dorset Regiment (Canadian Inf Battalion)	
			1/1st Bn. Hereford Regt. relieved 31st Canadian Infantry Battalion.	
			and took over Left Sub-sector of COLOGNE BRIDGEHEAD.	
			During the month recreational training was carried out in the afternoons, and the evenings were taken up by organised dances, concerts, etc.	

Emmy Thomas
Brigadier-General,
Commanding 102nd Infantry Brigade.

SECRET.

102ND INFANTRY BRIGADE ORDER NO. 1

APP. 1

Reference Map, NAMUR, 1/100.000
GERMANY SH. 2 L. 1/100.000

-----

1. The 34th Division will relieve the 2nd Canadian Division in the Right Sector of the Cologne Bridgehead.

2. (a) The 102nd Infantry Brigade Group composed of Units as under will relieve the 6th Canadian Infantry Brigade.
    102nd Infantry Brigade.
    208th Field Company R.E.
    No. 3 Company Train.
    102nd Field Ambulance.

    (b) Entrainment will be carried out in accordance with Table "Z" attached. Units will proceed independently to entraining Station.

3. Units of the 102nd Infantry Brigade Group on arrival at the COLOGNE Bridgehead will come under the command of G.O.C. 2nd Canadian Division until the command of the right Sector passes to G.O.C. 34th Division at 10.00 hours on 24th January. Officers Commanding Units will take over all defence ~~schemes~~ duties, Guard Post Orders and defence schemes from the Units they relieve.

4. Administrative instructions will be issued separately.

5. ACKNOWLEDGE.

                                    Captain,
                                    Brigade Major,
                                    102nd Infantry Brigade.

Distribution:-
Copy No. 1.   G.O.C.
                B.M.
                S.C.
                1/4th Bn. Cheshire Regt.
                1/7th Bn. Cheshire Regt.
                1/1st Bn. Hereford Regt.
                208th Field Coy. R.E.
                No. 3 Company Train.
                Brigade Supply Officer.
                102nd Field Ambulance.

TABLE "Z" to accompany 102nd Infantry Brigade Order No. 1

Ser. No.	Unit.	Date.	From	To	Relieving	Entraining Statn.	Time of Departure of Train.	Remarks.
1.	102nd Inf.Bde.H.Q. Signal Section. 102nd F.A.	21/1/1919	FOSSE	To 'G' Sub-area. Exact location to be notified later.		AUVELAIS.		Motor Ambulances will move by road.
2.	208th Fd.Coy.R.E. No 3 Coy. TRAIN	22/1/1919	LeVES NEVREMONT.	do.	UNITS OF 6th CANADIAN INF. BDE.	do	TO BE NOTIFIED LATER.	All Fd.Coys. will be accommodated at BONN on arrival and will move to TROISDORS at a late date.
3.	1/4th Bn.Cheshire Rgt. (less 1 Coy.Cooker and team) and Divl.Reception Camp.	22/1/1919.	AESEMONT & VITRIVAL.	do.		TAMINES		Will relieve 29th Canadian Inf.Batt. in the outpost line on arrival.
4.	1/7th Bn.Cheshire Rgt.	22/1/1919.	FOSSE.	do.		AUVELAIS.		
5.	1/1st Bn. Hereford Rgt.	23/1/1919.	FOSSE.	do.		do.		
6.	1 Cooker and Team of 1/4th Bn.Cheshire Rgt.	23/1/1919	TAMINES.	do.		TAMINES.		

Transport will be at entraining station 3 hours before schedule time for departure of train.
Personnel   do.   do.   1½   do.   do.
Detraining Stations not yet known.

War Diary

SECRET. 15
COPY No.....

APP II

102nd INFANTRY BRIGADE ORDER NO. 2

Reference Map:
   GERMANY 1/100,000 2 L. and
   TRACING attached.

1.   The 34th Division will be relieved of Sub-Sectors "A" and "B" of the Xth Corps Sector of the COLOGNE Bridgehead and will take over Sub-Sector "D" from the 41st Division.

2.   The 102nd Infantry Brigade Group will be relieved by the 14th Infantry Brigade Group consisting of :-
      14th Infantry Brigade.
      90th Field Ambulance.
      No. 3 Coy. 32nd Div. Train.
The relief will take place in accordance with the attached Table "A".
On relief, the 102nd Infantry Brigade Group will move by March Route and relieve the 103rd Infantry Brigade Group in "D" Sub-Sector.

3.   The following Advance Parties will proceed to the new area on Tuesday, January 28th to arrange details of relief and take over billets from 123rd Infantry Brigade.

102nd Infantry Brigade H.Q.	1 Officer, 1 O.R.
Each Battalion.	1 Officer, 1 O.R. H.Q.
	1 N.C.O. & men per Coy.
102nd Field Ambulance.	1 N.C.O.
No. 3 Coy. Train.	1 N.C.O.

   The Advance Party will proceed by lorries, details of which will be issued later.

4.   The Advance Party will be responsible for ~~making~~ *arranging* details regarding the taking over all defence and administrative duties and take over, check, and sign for all Guard Post Orders, Defence Schemes, Maps, Area Stores etc., from Units of the 123rd Infantry Brigade.
   Units will likewise hand over all such duties etc. to the incoming units of the 14th Infantry Brigade.
   In both cases receipts will be forwarded to Brigade H.Q. within 24th hours of the arrival of the unit concerned.

5.   Completion of relief will be wired to Brigade Headquarters as soon as possible.

6.   102nd Infantry Brigade Headquarters will close at OBER CASSEL at 10.00 hrs on February 1st and open at WAHN on arrival.

7.   ACKNOWLEDGE.

                       Captain,
                       A/Brigade Major,
27/1/19.   102nd Infantry Brigade.

DISTRIBUTION :

G.O.C.	1/4th Bn. Cheshire Regt.	No. 3 Coy. Train.
B.M.	1/7th Bn. Cheshire Regt.	101st Inf. Bde.
S.C.	1/1st Bn. Hereford Regt.	103rd Inf. Bde.
34th Div.	102nd Field Ambulance.	14th Inf. Bde.
		123rd Inf. Bde.

TABLE 'A' to accompany 102nd INFANTRY BRIGADE ORDER NO. 2.

Date.	Serial No.	UNIT.	From	To	Relieved by	Relieves	Remarks.
Jan.30th.	1.	1/1st Hereford Regt.	BEUEL	SIEGBURG PRISON.			To Billets vacated by 1/1st Herefords.
	2.	1/4th Cheshire Regt.	OBER CASSEL.	BEUEL.	'A' Bn. 14th I.Bde.		
Jan. 31st.	3.	1/1st Hereford Regt.	SIEGBURG PRISON.	SEELSCHEID.		'A' Bn. 123rd Coys.for Outpost line Inf.Brigade. will move by lorry.	
	4.	1/4th Cheshire Regt.	BEUEL.	SIEGBURG PRISON.	'B' Bn.14th I.Bde.	'B' Bn. 123rd Inf. Brigade.	
	5.	1/7th Cheshire Regt.	BEUEL.	LOHMAN		139th F.A.	
	6.	102nd Field Ambulance.	BEUEL.	WAHN BARRACKS.	90 th F.A.	No.3 Coy. 41st Div.Train.	
	7.	No.3 Coy.Div.Train.	BEUEL.	WAHN.	No.2 Coy.32nd Div.Train.		
Feb. 1st.	8.	1/4th Cheshire Regt.	SIEGBURG PRISON.	LIND.		'C' Bn. 123rd Inf.Brigade.	Command 'A' Sub-Sector passes to G.O.C. 14th Inf. Bde. at 10.00.
	9.	102nd Inf.Bde.H.Q.	OBER CASSEL.	WAHN			Command of 'D' Sub-Sector passes to G.O.C 102nd Inf.Bde.at 10.00 hours.
Feb. 2nd.	10.	102nd Inf.Bde.H.Q.		WAHN		123rd Bde. Headquarters.	

102 Inf Bde

Army Form C. 2118.

WAR DIARY
or
INTELLIGENCE SUMMARY.

(Erase heading not required.)

Reference Map 1/100,000
GERMANY M J 36

Instructions regarding War Diaries and Intelligence Summaries are contained in F.S. Regs., Part II. and the Staff Manual respectively. Title pages will be prepared in manuscript.

Place	Date	Hour	Summary of Events and Information	Remarks and references to Appendices
WAHN	1/2/19		Relief of 4th Division continued in accordance with Brigade Order No 2	App No 1
"			See Bde Diary January	
"	2/2/19		Brigade Headquarters moved from OBER-CASSEL to WAHN	
"			Italian sector "D" of Cologne Bridgehead outpost line	
"	3/2/19		Brigade Headquarters moved to LOHMAR	
LOHMAR	4/2/19		Holding outpost line	
"	5/2/19		Brigade Summary Order No 3 issued	App No 2
"	6/2/19		Brigade Order No 3 issued	App No 3
"	7/2/19		Relieved in "D" sector of Outpost line by 101st Infantry Brigade in accordance with Brigade Order No 3	
"			Brigade HQ moved to SIEGBURG	
SIEGBURG	8/2/19 – 13.2.19		Training + Guard duties	
	14.2.19		do	
	15.2.19		Brig Gen Cunningham proceeds to Brigade	
			Divisional Commander returns to Brigade	
	16.2.19		Lt Col Evans McCurdy 1/1st Res Herts R assumes command of Brigade was	
			Brig Gen Jellicoe CMG DSO on leave to UK	

Army Form C. 2118.

WAR DIARY
or
INTELLIGENCE SUMMARY.
(Erase heading not required.)

Place	Date	Hour	Summary of Events and Information	Remarks and references to Appendices
SIEGBURG	7-2-19 to 28.2.19		Training & Guards duties.	

Erasmus Williams
Brig Gen
Commdg 102nd Infantry Brigade

HQ 2 Eastern Sixty Bde

WAR DIARY
or
INTELLIGENCE SUMMARY
(Erase heading not required.)

Army Form C. 2118.

REFERENCE MAP.
GERMANY SH. 2. 1/100,000

M / 39

Place	Date	Hour	Summary of Events and Information	Remarks and references to Appendices
SIEGBURG	1919 Mar 1		1/7th Bn. Cheshire Regt. left 102nd Infantry Brigade to join 1st Division	
"	Mar 3rd		52nd Bn Bedford's Regt. joined 102nd Infantry Brigade & were billeted at SIEGBURG	
"	Mar 6th		G.O.C. Division inspected the 52nd Battn. Bedfordshire Regt. at SIEGBURG	
"	Mar 13th		G.O.C. 2nd Army inspected 52nd Battn. Bedfordshire Regt. at SIEGBURG	
"			Brig Gen. E. Williams C.M.G. D.S.O. returned from leave in England & resumed command of the Brigade vice R. Col Evans 1/7 Bn. Hertfordshire Regt.	
"	Mar 14th		52nd Bn. Sussex Regt. arrived at SIEGBURG temporarily attached to 102nd Infantry Brigade	
			1/7th Bn. Hertfordshire Regt. disbanded as follows. Volunteers retained to Divisional Pioneers & 4th Bn. Suffolk Regt. Balance Cadre & demobilisable Men to Divisional Reception Camp SIEGBURG	
"	Mar 15th		Capt. A.B. Locks M.C. Staff Capt admitted to hospital	
"	Mar 16th		Brigade Order No 4 issued with reference to arrival of 53rd Battn. Bedfordshire Regt.	APP. 1
"	Mar 17th		G.O.C. 2nd Army inspected 52nd Bn. Sussex Regt. at SIEGBURG	

Army Form C. 2118.

WAR DIARY
or
INTELLIGENCE SUMMARY.
(Erase heading not required.)

REFERENCE MAP
GERMANY. SHEET 22. 1/100,000

Instructions regarding War Diaries and Intelligence Summaries are contained in F. S. Regs., Part II. and the Staff Manual respectively. Title pages will be prepared in manuscript.

Place	Date	Hour	Summary of Events and Information	Remarks and references to Appendices
SIEGBURG	1919 Mar 18th		53rd Bn. Bedfordshire R arrived at SIEGBURG & came under Command of 102nd Inft Bde.	
"	Mar 22nd		Brigade Order No 5 issued, with reference to move of 1/4th Bn. Ches. Regt.	APP 2.
"	Mar 23rd		1/4th Bn. Cheshire Regt. left WAHN by train to join 1st Division	
"	Mar 24th		51st Bn. Bedfordshire Regt arrived at LIND Barracks from ENGLAND 102nd Infantry Brigade Eastern Division now Composed as under:- 51st Bn. Bedfordshire Regt. (Graduated Battalion) 52nd Bn. " " do 53rd Bn. " " (Young Soldier Battalion)	
"	Mar 26		Brig. Gen. H.C.Jackson (from 50th Division) assumed Command of 102nd Infantry Brigade vice Brig Gen. E.Gillam C.M.G. D.S.O. to Divisional I/c A.S. in Command of Divisional Cadres	

E Jackson Bng.
Brig Genl
Com. manding 2nd Infantry Brigade

To, Adjutant General,

Base.

[STAMP: CENTRAL REGISTRY HEADQUARTERS WIMEREUX 17 MAY 1919]

BM/1/1.

No.

Herewith War Diary for Month of April.

[signature]
Brigadier General,
Commanding, 2nd Infantry Brigade.

13/5/1919.

Army Form C. 2118.

WAR DIARY
or
INTELLIGENCE SUMMARY.
(Erase heading not required.)

HEADQRS. 2ND INFY BRIGADE
EASTERN. DIV.

Instructions regarding War Diaries and Intelligence Summaries are contained in F. S. Regs., Part II. and the Staff Manual respectively. Title pages will be prepared in manuscript.

REFERANCE MAP.
GERMANY S.H. & L. 1/100,000

Place	Date	Hour	Summary of Events and Information	Remarks and references to Appendices
SIEGBURG	April 1st		Platoon, Company and Recreational Training of three New Battalions commenced.	
"	" 3rd		G.O.C. Division inspected the 52nd Bn Bedfordshire Reg. at LIND.	
"	" 7th		G.O.C. Army inspected 57th Bn Bedfordshire Reg. at LIND.	
"	" 8th		The Battalion 52nd Bn Bedfordshire Reg. commenced work on new 400 yd range on SIEGBURG – LOHMAR Road. Working party found daily by 52nd & 53rd Bns Bedfordshire Reg. alternately	
"	" 12th		G.O.C. Division inspected the 2nd Inf Brigade in Parade at SIEGBURG. Major Tallent's D.S.O. Lancashire Fus. assumed duties of Brigade Major vice Capt M. Carr M.C. P. Scot Fus appointed Staff Capt.	
"	" 15th		52nd Batt. Bedfordshire Reg. returns 6th Bn R.W. Kent Reg. as Left Battn in Right Brigade Sector Hyacinth I of Eastern Div. Perimeter Line. Lt. Col. W.A. ATKINSON. D.S.O. Bedfordshire Reg. assumed command of 51st/53rd Bedfordshire Reg. vice Lt. Col H.W. Gush D.S.O. M.C.	I
"	" 16		Bt. Col. R.D.F. OLDMAN C.M.G. D.S.O. NORFOLK REGT. assumed command of 53rd Bn Bedfordshire Reg. vice Col W.F. BARKER C.M.G. D.S.O.	
"	" 17		57th Batt. Bedfordshire Reg. relieved 10th Bn R.W. Kent Reg. as Right Battn in Right Brigade Sector of Eastern Div. Perimeter Line.	I
"	"		2nd Infantry Bde. H.Q. moved to ALLNER in relief of 1st Inf. Bde.	I

Army Form C. 2118.

WAR DIARY
or
INTELLIGENCE SUMMARY.
(Erase heading not required.)

Instructions regarding War Diaries and Intelligence Summaries are contained in F. S. Regs., Part II. and the Staff Manual respectively. Title pages will be prepared in manuscript.

Place	Date	Hour	Summary of Events and Information	Remarks and references to Appendices
SIEGBURG	April 17		G.O.C. 2nd Inf. Bde assumed command of Right Brigade Sector of Eastern Sub. Perimeter Line	Appendix I
			Lt Col W.R. MANN D.S.O. Bedfordshire Regt assumed command of 2nd Bedfordshire Regt vice	
			Lt Col W.N.R. Gilbert-Cooper.	
ALLNER	" 17		Brigadier held conference on Subject of Defence Scheme - Following officers present	
			O.C's Infty Batts - O.C. 152 Brigade R.F.A. - O.C. A Coy 34 MG Bn - O.C. 207 Field Coy RE - Bde Major - Staff Cpt	
	" 18		Brigadier accompanied by Bde Major and O.C. 207 Field Coy RE inspected Southern Half	
			of frontline of Resistance	
	" 19		2nd Brigade Defence Scheme Issued	Appendix II
	" 20		Church Parades. Bde Major visited Southern half of Perimeter line	
			Their Majesties the King & Queen of Belgium accompanied by the Corps and Div'l	
			Commanders visited Brigade H.Q. for Tea.	
	" 29		The G.O.C. C. in C. inspected the 5-3"B" Bedfordshire Regt on parade at	
			SIEGBURG. The Corps Commander and the Div'l Commander were present	

Walker Major B.M.
BRIGADIER GENERAL.
102ND INFANTRY BRIGADE.

Army Form C. 2118.

WAR DIARY
INTELLIGENCE SUMMARY

HEADQRS. 2ND INFY BDE EASTERN DIV

REF. MAP. COL N 1:50,000

Place	Date	Hour	Summary of Events and Information	Remarks and references to Appendices
ALLNER	MAY 1		Tactical Exercise held to practise Manning Battle Stations - Brigade took part and also 152 Bde R.F.A. - A Coy Mx Corps - 207 Field Coy R.E.	
"	2		Conference of Comdg Officers at Bde Headquarters. The conference was partly on the Tactical Exercise of the previous day and partly on general subjects.	
"	8		Tactical Exercise held to practise manning a position facing North (viz. left flank). Brigade units only took part.	
"	9		Field Marshall H.R.H. The Duke of Connaught K.G. etc. visited the Brigade area. Visited billets etc of 51st Bn Bedfordshire Regt at HENNEF then deferred in the area of The Battn, finally having tea at Brigade Headquarters. Guard of Honour was found by 51st Bn Bedfordshire Regt. Commander - Major G. WHITE M.C. - Guard 2 other officers and 100 Rank and File with Drums - H.R.H. expressed himself as pleased with the appearance of the Guard.	
"	10		Conference of Adjutants held at Brigade Headquarters under the Presidency of the Brigade Major.	

Page 2
Army Form C. 2118.

HEADQRS 2nd INFY. BDE. WAR DIARY
EASTERN DIV
INTELLIGENCE SUMMARY.

(Erase heading not required.)

Instructions regarding War Diaries and Intelligence Summaries are contained in F.S. Regs., Part II. and the Staff Manual respectively. Title pages will be prepared in manuscript.

REF: MAP COLN 1/250,000

Place	Date	Hour	Summary of Events and Information	Remarks and references to Appendices
ALLNER	MAY 10		2nd Brigade Light Tench Motor Battery formed. Located at HENNEF. Commander. Capt. G.S. DEXTER. 51st Bn Bedfordshire Regt — 1 Officer and 11 O.R. from 51st Bn Bedfordshire Regt — 1 Officer and 14 O.R. from 52nd Bn Bedfordshire Regt — 1 Officer and 14 O.R. from 53rd Bn Bedfordshire Regt	
"	11		Church Parades.	
"	15		Eastern Div Staff Ride to test Signal communication in open warfare	
"	17		Conference of Commdg. Officers at Bde H.Q. on general subjects	
"	18		Church Parades	
"	22		Commander in Chief visits Brigade area. Was conducted to several observation points by Brigadier	
"	23		Brigade Order No. 7 issued. Instructions for possible advance into Germany issued.	Appendix I.
"	29		Conference held at Bde Headqrs on the subject of possible advance. Present. OC.s 51st, 52nd, 53rd Bedfordshire Regt, A Coy 34 M.G. Batt., 102 Field Ambulance, No. 4 Coy Div Train, 207 Field Coy R.E. Bde Major & Staff Captain.	

Gallen Major BM
2nd Inf Bde
for BGC
2nd Inf Bde

2nd Bde

Army Form C. 2118.

HEADQRS. 2ND INFY BDE
EASTERN DIVN.

Instructions regarding War Diaries and Intelligence
Summaries are contained in F.S. Regs., Part II.
and the Staff Manual respectively. Title pages
will be prepared in manuscript.

WAR DIARY
or
INTELLIGENCE SUMMARY.
(Erase heading not required.)

Place	Date	Hour	Summary of Events and Information	Remarks and references to Appendices
ALLNER	JUNE 2	3 P.M.	Corps Comdr (X Corps) visited training during the morning.	
"	6		Brigade Novices Boxing Tournament held at HENNEF	
"	8		Major G.S. Tallents D.S.O. left the Brigade to take up appointment as G.S.O.2 G.H.Q	
	9		Divisional Commander visited B.G.C. in afternoon.	
	11		Brigade Horse Show. Championship Cup won by 57" Bedfordshire Regt.	
	12,13,14.		G.O.C. inspected Ration Dumps and inspected billets of 51"&53" Bedfordshire Regts. Training	
	15		Div Commander visited Brigade Commander in his H/Quarters	
	16		Brigade Commander visited Battn Commanders	
	17		Telephone message 07.15 hours from Division saying J day would be Friday 20th confirmed by wire 09.00 hours later warned by phone 06.00 hours. Confirmed by wire 09.15 hours. Bde Instruction No 7 issued	appendix I.
	18		51" Bedfords Athletic Sports on Show Ground. Major Gen The Marquis of Salisbury K.G. visited the Brigade. Brigade Instruction Nº 8 & 9 issued	appendix II & III
	19		J - 1 day. 51" Bedfords evacuated HENNEF which was occupied by Hd 1st E. Brigade and concentrated at ALLNER and BROL 52nd Bedfords concentrated B.6 & B Coys.	

D. D. & L., London, E.C.
(A7833) Wt. W809/M1672 550,000 4/17 Sch. 52a Forms/C/2118/14

Army Form C. 2118.

WAR DIARY
or
INTELLIGENCE SUMMARY.
(Erase heading not required.)

Instructions regarding War Diaries and Intelligence Summaries are contained in F. S. Regs., Part II. and the Staff Manual respectively. Title pages will be prepared in manuscript.

Place	Date	Hour	Summary of Events and Information	Remarks and references to Appendices
	June			
ALLNER	19.		at SELIGENTHAL and KALTZAVEN A Coy on Outpost line. They postponed.	
	22.		C in C visits Brigade H.Q. during the afternoon.	
	24.		Brigadier inspected the 3 Batts of the Brigade during the day.	
	25.		Advance Parties from troops proceeded to WAHN	
	26.		Brigadier Gen H.C. Jackson C.B. D.S.O. proceeded on leave to the U.K.	
			Lt. Col W Allason D.S.O. assumed command of the Brigade	
	28.		Peace Declared	Appendix "I"
			Bde note NO 1 issued	
	29.		Bde Order NO 1 issued	" "I"
	30.		51st and 52nd Bedfords relieved in the outpost line by the 1st Brigade	
			63rd Bedfords marched to WAHN from SIEGBURG arriving 1700 hrs	

W Allason
Lieut Col
Comdg 2nd East Inf Bde

Army Form C. 2118.

WAR DIARY
or
INTELLIGENCE SUMMARY.

(Erase heading not required.)

of 2nd Eastern Infantry Bde. H.Q.

Instructions regarding War Diaries and Intelligence Summaries are contained in F.S. Regs., Part II. and the Staff Manual respectively. Title pages will be prepared in manuscript.

Place	Date	Hour	Summary of Events and Information	Remarks and references to Appendices
WAHN	JULY 1		51st and 52nd Bedfordshire Regt: proceeded from HENNEF and KALDAUEN to P. of W. Camp WAHN. Brigade H.Q. opened at WAHN.	
	3.		General Holiday to celebrate conclusion of Peace	
	4.		2nd Class Army Certificate of Instruction Exams held, 336 men sat from Brigade	
	5.		" " " " " " ", 1539 " " " "	
	6.		Brigade Church Parade, Special unites Thanksgiving service to celebrate signature of Peace.	
	7th		Butts. at Coy and Batt Training	
	11.		" " " "	
	12.		Brigadier Genl. H.C. Jackson C.B., D.S.O. returned from leave and resumed command of this Brigade.	
	14.		Battle Training	
	16.		Trip on the Rhine 700 men from Brigade spent the day on the Rhine.	
	18.		Brigade Tactical Scheme	
	19.		General Holiday.	

Army Form C. 2118.

WAR DIARY
or
INTELLIGENCE SUMMARY.

(Erase heading not required.)

Place	Date	Hour	Summary of Events and Information	Remarks and references to Appendices
WAHN.	July 21.		Officers of Bedfordshire Bgde. Dinner at the Casino under the presidency of Brigadier Genl. H.C. Jackson.	
	22.		Brigade Tactical Exercise. Exam: matrices for Army Certificate of Education (22-24) 50 men in Brigade sat.	
	24.		Brigade Athletic Sports Championship Cups won by the 5th Bedfordshire Regt.	
	25.		Battalion Training	
	28.		Three Buses of Brigade inspected by B.G.C. Brigade memorial Service in the afternoon at the garrison Chapel in memory of the Officers and men of the Bedfordshire Regt. who fell in the War 1914-1918.	
	29		Brigade Tactical Exercise	
	31.		Eastern Div Horse Show. Brigadier Gen H.C. Jackson C.B, DSO recalled to England on a Special mission. But Col R.D.F. OLDMAN C.M.G., D.S.O. assumed command of the Brigade. By command of H.H. the King, the Bedfordshire Regt. will infuture be known as the Bedfordshire and Hertfordshire Regt.	

Col.
Comdg. 2nd Eastern Inf. Bde.

R.D.F. Oldman

www.ingramcontent.com/pod-product-compliance
Lightning Source LLC
Chambersburg PA
CBHW080853230426
43662CB00013B/2090